Entertainment

The Information Revolution

ENTERTAINMENT

WALTER OLEKSY

Facts On File, Inc.
AN INFOBASE HOLDINGS COMPANY

Entertainment

Copyright © 1996 by Walter Oleksy

All rights reserved. No part of this book may be reproduced or utilized in any form or by any means, electronic or mechanical, including photocopying, recording, or by any information storage or retrieval systems, without permission in writing from the publisher. For information contact:

Facts On File, Inc.
11 Penn Plaza
New York, NY 10001

Library of Congress Cataloging-in-Publication Data

Oleksy, Walter G., 1930–

    Entertainment / Walter Oleksy.
      p. cm. — (The information revolution)
    Includes bibliographical references.
    Summary: Provides an overview of how the entertainment industry is being revolutionized by new developments in electronics such as digital wide-screen television, laser disc players, computer movies, and interactive CD-ROM.
    ISBN 0-8160-3077-4 (acid-free paper)
    1. Home entertainment systems. 2. Information technology—Social aspects. [1. Technology—Social aspects. 2. Electronics.]
I. Title. II. Series.
TK7881.3.054   1996
384—dc20   96-22110

The Information Revolution series offers young adult readers an introductory survey of exciting recent developments in information technology such as laser disks, CD-ROMS, and on-line libraries. Each book in the series explores the practical applications of new technology in a particular field of endeavor, from medicine to education, from business to entertainment. Taken together, the books in the series provide students with a clear and insightful view of the ways in which information technology is changing how we live and work.

Facts On File books are available at special discounts when purchased in bulk quantities for businesses, associations, institutions or sales promotions. Please call our Special Sales Department in New York at 212/967-8800 or 800/322-8755.

Text design by Catherine Hyman
Jacket design by Nora Wertz

This book is printed on acid-free paper.

Printed in the United States of America

MP FOF 10 9 8 7 6 5 4 3 2 1

CONTENTS

	Introduction: You and the Information Revolution	VII
1	Entertainment on the Information Superhighway	1
2	Television—Satellite, High-Definition, Interactive, and 3-D TV	9
3	VCRs and Videotapes	19
4	Video Games Tekkies Play	25
5	Multimedia and Interactive Technology	32
6	Virtual Reality at the Movies	44
7	That's Edutainment!	52
8	Look, Ma, I'm On-line!	61
9	Movie Magic: Digital Special Effects	67
10	Home Theaters	73
11	Rock Goes Interactive	79
12	Radio's Role in the Information Revolution	86
13	Interactive Sports Technology—A Whole New Ballgame	92
14	Privacy, Piracy, and Pranks in the Information Age	98
15	What's Ahead in Entertainment?	103
16	The Future of the Information Revolution	108
	Glossary	111
	Sources	116
	Index	121

Introduction

YOU AND THE INFORMATION REVOLUTION

American business, industry, government, and education have already become actively engaged in a new information revolution proposed and encouraged by President Bill Clinton and Vice President Al Gore shortly after their inauguration early in 1993. They call the new technological concept an "electronic data superhighway," a vast communications system designed to revolutionize data gathering and distribution. Similar in concept to telephone lines that link phone users along a "telephone superhighway," fiber optic telephone lines or satellite transmissions would link computers in homes, schools, businesses, banks, research centers, universities, libraries, hospitals, and other outlets by two-way interactive multimedia data, sound, and video.

The Clinton administration wants the United States to take the lead in developing and producing new technology to implement the data superhighway. It could revitalize industry, stimulate the economy, and put the United States in the forefront of worldwide technological competitiveness. The ambitious vision calls for using government-backed research projects, tax

> The data superhighway would bring America into direct competition with Japan, France, Germany, and other nations competing for an edge in the technology race, and put more Americans back to work in skilled, high-paying jobs.

incentives, and trade policy to help high-tech industries become engines of economic growth and job creation.

The data superhighway would bring America into direct competition with Japan, France, Germany, and other nations competing for an edge in the technology race, and put more Americans back to work in skilled, high-paying jobs. By enhancing the gathering and dissemination of information, digital technology is already achieving far-reaching effects in education and learning, business and industry, science and medicine, and entertainment and other fields.

Students are using home or school computers to access distant databases at universities and other institutions, thus enabling them to work with educators in other cities and countries, and communicate and interact with educational materials displayed as integrated text, sound, and video on computers or televisions.

Businesses are sending computer drawings and other information between distant points to speed design and manufacture of new products. Advanced teleconferencing linking computers with telephones, video recorders, and television sets, can enable business and industry to conduct electronic meetings of people in distant cities, and similarly link classrooms with university lecture halls, museums, libraries, etc.

Scientists and researchers would be able to exchange vast amounts of written, audio, and visual data regardless of where they are located, working together more efficiently and achieving greater shared knowledge, thus speeding up otherwise lengthy research projects and avoiding duplication of study.

Individuals can work, study, shop at home, and enjoy new forms of entertainment through the interaction of television, video recorders, computers, and laser technology. Building a data superhighway will speed the pace at which business and industry switch from military to domestic, peacetime research and development of existing and new products. Billions of government research and development funds could be transferred from military to civilian commercial uses. Biotechnology, robotics, artificial intelligence, digital imaging, and data storage are some of the areas that would benefit. Another major benefit of the new information revolution

> Individuals can work, study, shop at home, and enjoy new forms of entertainment through the interaction of television, video recorders, computers, and laser technology.

also offers is to give new hope and direction to America's high school and college students in finding skilled and high-paying jobs related to the new technology.

The information revolution is already on-line because of new inventions such as the early stages of digital and wireless telecommunications, fiber optics, and interactive audio and video technology. The goal is to enhance productivity by seamlessly moving vast quantities of digital data such as sound, graphics, and video over high-capacity networks between universities, corporations, industrial research centers, health-care facilities, and ultimately every home and classroom.

In this series of books on the new information revolution, author Walter Oleksy has interviewed technology specialists in business and industry, science and medicine, and entertainment, as well as students and their teachers in electronic classrooms who are actively using much of the new technology. By joining them (so to speak) in these pages, you will learn more about the new technologies and the profound effects the developing electronic data superhighway will have on your life.

Little over a decade ago, while tinkering in the California garage of one of their parents, two young men barely out of college invented and then marketed the Apple computer, which soon developed into a phenomenon and made them millionaires while bringing personal computers to the world. By learning about and using the new technology, you could be the next big player in one of the most exciting and potentially rewarding of futures—the electronic revolution that will speed us into the interactive multimedia age.

—Peter W. Frey,
Professor of Psychology, Northwestern University
Senior Research Scientist, Pattern Recognition Systems, Inc.,
Evanston, Illinois

Entertainment

Entertainment on the Information Superhighway

Like the high-tech, super-fast action of today's multimedia and interactive video arcade and computer CD-ROM games, technology in entertainment is moving and changing at hyperdrive speed. It is almost impossible to keep up with what is being offered to the public today in technology-enhanced movies, video recording, computers and game software, laser and CD-ROM disks, music, and network, cable, and satellite television. What the future holds, beyond the next few years and into the 21st century, is still beyond imagining. Two things, however, are predictable: New technology is going to make entertainment even more exciting and fun.

The growth of home entertainment technology continues at a rapid pace, according to January 1995 figures compiled by LINK Resources Corporation, a market research company in New York City. Nearly 24.5 million color television sets were sold in 1994,

Multimedia personal computers are in the homes of more than six million Americans.
(Photo courtesy of I.B.M.)

making the total number of sets in American homes 215 million. Some 11.9 million videocassette recorders were sold that same year, for a total of 114 million VCRs in homes across the country.

Among the newest technologies, multimedia personal computers accounted for slightly over four million units sold in 1994, for a total of nearly six million in American homes. Laser disk player sales reached 278,000, bringing the total number of machines capable of playing 12-inch disks to 1.44 million. Some 6.46 million computers equipped with CD-ROM drives were sold in 1994, for a total of nearly 10 million in homes.

About 22,000 8-bit video game players were sold in 1994, bringing their total in American homes to 32.5 million. Sales of 16-bit players reached 10.2 million in 1994, for a total of 33.8 million in current home use. Some 4.4 million units of handheld video game players such as Lynx, GameBoy, and Game Gear, were sold in 1994 for a total of 24.1 million.

Exciting glimpses into what the future holds in entertainment were on view and were demonstrated at the 1995 Summer Consumer Electronics Show in Chicago. The emphasis was on multimedia—the combined use of computer, television, laser disk, and other technology for super-realistic sight and sound experiences.

At the city's gigantic lakefront exhibition hall, McCormick Place, the latest video recorders, disk players, big screen and wide screen television sets, and satellite dishes amazed even those who diligently follow media reports for the latest in entertainment technology.

The show overflowed to the Chicago Hilton hotel where the latest advances in music and movie sound systems, shown with video demonstrations, gave video and audio buffs exciting glimpses into those futures. Even for those who keep up with and purchase the latest audio and video equipment, the convention was like stepping into a multimedia, interactive hyperdrive future.

But you don't have to go to a national consumer electronics show to see how wide and significant electronic information technology in entertainment has become in American life. This is clearly evident both inside and outside of the home, as reported by the Times Mirror Center for the People and the Press in its 1994 survey, "Technology in the American Household."

Nearly one in three households owns a personal computer, and about 23 million adults use a home computer every day. About 28 percent of young people use a computer at home for schoolwork or to play educational games, and 46 percent of teenagers have a home computer. Males tend to use computers more than females, but that statistic changes with the younger generations. Of today's young people using home computers, 46 percent are girls and 53 percent are boys.

More than one in ten households (12 percent) use a modem-equipped computer. As many as 6 percent of all Americans, or 11 million people, go "on-line," communicating via computer and telephone. Half that number are connected to commercial information services, such as Prodigy, or to electronic bulletin boards.

An interesting finding of the report was that most computer and other high-tech users are not "nerds." The survey debunked the stereotype that portrays technologically advanced people as less outgoing, socially skilled, or athletic than average. Those who use a computer at home regularly or go on-line were as likely as other people from similar backgrounds to say they go out "a lot" or participate in athletics. Further, they were more likely than their less technologically experienced counterparts to be club or association members and were also more likely to describe their personalities as "outgoing."

Although much of the Times Mirror study focused on the penetration of computer technology into everyday life, it was noted that the most dramatic piece of personal technology is still the television set. Like computers, television sets are becoming increasingly more powerful and adaptable for other entertainment uses.

In what was cited as the most significant discovery of the study, only 7 percent of the television sets in American homes are used

Eleven million Americans are communicating with each other by going "on-line," using computers connected to a modem and telephone.
(Photo courtesy of I.B.M.)

exclusively for watching broadcast television programs. Some 93 percent of TV sets are attached to cable programming converter boxes, Sega or Nintendo game-playing machines, VCRs, or satellite broadcast dishes.

One out of six Americans watched a movie, concert, or sporting event at home via a pay-per-view service offered by a cable company.

> Only 7 percent of the television sets in American homes are used exclusively for watching broadcast television programs.

Traditional large-size satellite dishes were providing television for nearly four million households nationwide. Meanwhile, another million Americans bought the new, smaller, and less expensive RCA Digital Satellite System (DSS), which offers 150 channels with laser-disk sharpness and CD-quality sound, while promising up to 500 channels in the near future.

Most Americans, by a 67 percent to 27 percent margin, prefer to watch a rented movie at home rather than go out to a theater, according to the Times Mirror report. The video store remains the preferred source for renting movies, even in households that subscribe to pay-per-view cable or satellite services. Only 6 percent of those surveyed say they prefer a pay-per-view movie on television over renting a video in a store.

Majorities of all ages and both sexes surveyed said they use their remote controls during commercials. Only 35 percent of TV viewers said they usually watch commercials. High school graduates watch a home shopping network more often than college graduates (33 percent vs. 19 percent).

Some 85 percent of all households surveyed reported having at least one VCR in the home. The vast majority of households, 64 percent, subscribe to cable television to receive more channels than are available locally and clearer reception than regular broadcast stations can provide. Twenty-eight percent of all households subscribe to premium services, such as HBO and Showtime,

> Television and computer industries are investing millions if not billions of dollars in the increasing war over which technology will provide the basic source of entertainment in the home.

which offer new movies, special sports, and music events for an extra monthly fee.

When asked which information technology—old or new—they would miss most if it were no longer available, 67 percent of those surveyed said it would be their daily newspaper. Next, 65 percent said they would miss their personal computer, and 63 percent their basic cable TV system. Fifty-three percent would miss their satellite dish, and 50 percent their computer modem. Somewhat fewer users would miss their VCR (43 percent) or fax machine (41 percent). The technology Americans would give up most readily is premium cable: Only 29 percent of those who subscribe say they would miss the service "a lot" if deprived of it.

What may change the results in future surveys of how and what information technology Americans use for entertainment is the growing battle between the television and computer industries. Both are investing millions if not billions of dollars in the increasing war over which technology will provide the basic source of entertainment in the home.

Television industry leaders maintain that television, not the personal computer, will be the medium to take full advantage of the many interactive services already available or coming in the near future. Among these are video games that can be played with someone in another location, home shopping, electronic mail, video conferencing, and news and information retrieval. These companies, including Time Warner, Telecommunications Inc., American Telephone and Telegraph (AT&T), US West, and Bell Atlantic, have invested millions of dollars in dozens of field tests for interactive television in places such as Orlando, Florida; Queens, New York; and Alexandria, Virginia.

On the other side, Nicholas Negroponte, director of the Media Laboratory at the Massachusetts Institute of Technology (MIT), predicts: "For interactive applications, the personal computer is going to win." His research organization, to remain impartial, receives financing from both the personal computer and television industries.

Those who bet on television as the best way to bring entertainment and other information technology into the home say it is because almost everyone has a TV and most people are more comfortable using a TV than a computer. Computer advocates refute this by pointing out that advances in personal computers are making them much easier to operate, more useful, and less expensive. For example, the newest generation of personal computers have chips powerful enough to run video with the same resolution and lack of jerkiness as a television picture. New computer technology already allows a full-length movie to be stored on one 5-inch CD-ROM disk, and further refinements may enable storing as many as three movies on one disk.

Many communications, computer, and entertainment companies that once believed television to be the best medium for showing video games and other technologies, have begun investing heavily in interactive services. They can be used on the personal computer instead of, or at least as well as, on the television. This change of mind comes because these companies believe that the future of electronic entertainment lies with the younger generation, which is more familiar and comfortable with computers.

Now that personal computers can offer video of television quality, many software publishers are producing entertainment and educational products that can be delivered over cable television networks and phone lines to personal computer users. Microsoft is developing interactive programs

> The future of electronic entertainment lies with the younger generation, which is more familiar and comfortable with computers.

ENTERTAINMENT ON THE INFORMATION SUPERHIGHWAY 7

including ones that allow viewers to gather sports statistics and conduct home banking. Prodigy, in cooperation with the ESPN cable network, plans to offer its users video clips of sports highlights.

It is also possible that the winner of the computer-television battle will not be one or the other technology but a marriage of the two. Multimedia and interactive game-playing machines and computer-driven software could be hooked up to new big–screen and wide-screen television sets. Also, a single device combining all the attributes of a computer and a television may emerge. It could have a high-definition screen and a controller that is a cross between a remote-control wand and a keyboard.

Whichever technology wins the TV-computer battle, or if a new one displaces them both, the real winner is the consumer. With billions of dollars being invested to determine who can produce the most hardware and software the fastest, the consumer will get technology that is user-friendly, interactive and inexpensive, providing the sharpest digital picture and best sound. All we need do is enjoy what there is now and look forward to what is yet to come.

2

Television-Satellite, High-Definition, Interactive, and 3-D TV

Satellite, High-Definition, and Interactive TV

Television has come a long way in the half-century since the first commercial sets were introduced in 1945 with high price tags and small screens. Five years after, there were 1.5 million TV sets in the U.S., and just a year later, 15 million. Today, according to LINK Resources, there are more than 215 million color TV sets in American homes.

In 1950, an hour-long television special featuring Ed Sullivan and Arthur Godfrey heralded the start of regular commercial color TV transmissions. A mere 18 years later, the first color TV transmission from space enabled viewers to see the Moon close-up, as *Apollo 10* astronauts orbited it in their spacecraft.

The first TV program broadcast in stereo, Johnny Carson's "Tonight Show," aired on July 27, 1984. The following May, NBC became the first network to distribute all its TV programs by satellite.

Television viewers thought they were tuning in to the best and the most when cable service began about 15 years ago, offering up to 30 channels and new movies for a monthly fee. Today, cable TV is in 64 percent of American homes. The vast majority of subscribers take only basic service for about $20 a month rather than paying additional fees for premium movie and special event channels.

Only 4 percent of respondents to a 1994 Times Mirror study reported they owned a satellite dish, which directs television signals to their homes from outer space. "Backyard satellite" systems, which have been around since the late 1970s, cost about $2,000. They receive an analog signal using an antenna 7 to 10 feet in diameter,

Thomson's Digital Satellite System is comprised of an 18-inch receiving dish, computerized TV set-top box, and remote control device. (Photo courtesy RCA)

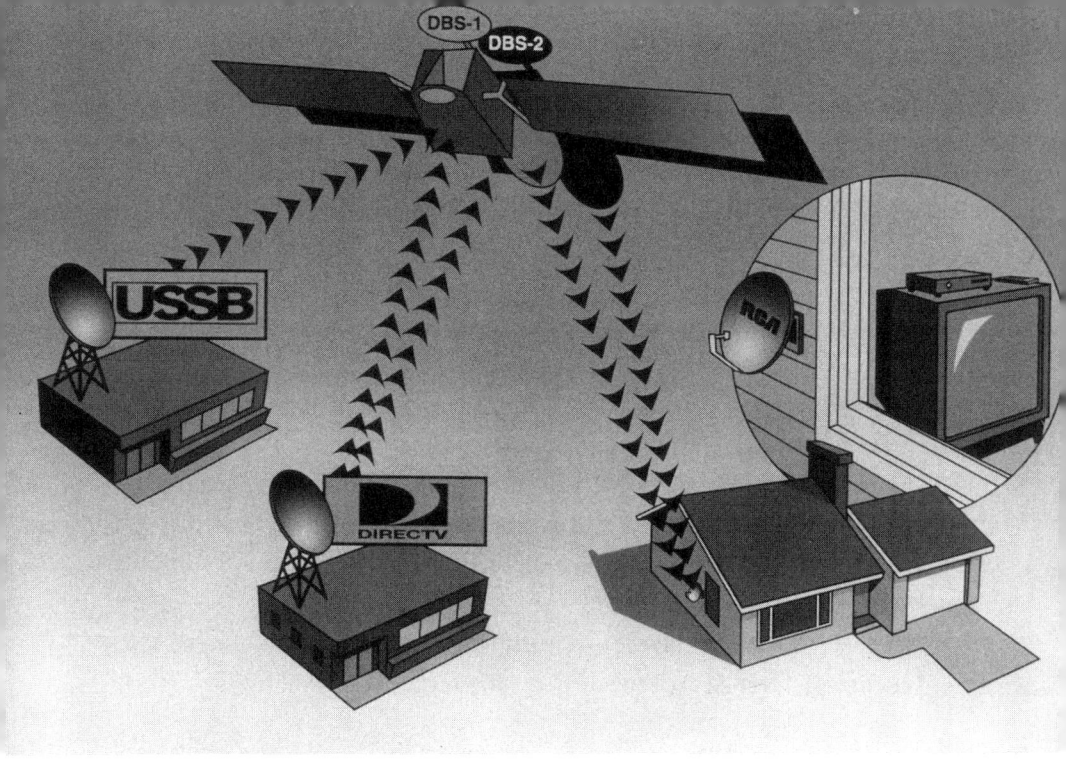

TV signals are sent from Earth-based stations to a satellite 22,300 miles in space, then relayed to homes. (Photo courtesy RCA)

and offer a much sharper picture and better sound than broadcast television.

The high price and large size of receiving dishes kept many people from investing in satellite TV until a new satellite system was introduced in 1994. RCA's Digital Satellite System (DSS), made by Thomson Consumer Electronics and using a much smaller 18-inch dish, was offered for about $700. During the first six months the system was for sale, it was sold to about half a million people.

The DSS system receives television signals from a satellite located 22,300 miles in space in geostationary orbit. It enables viewers to watch 150 channels in laser-disk sharpness and CD-quality sound, with a promise of as many as 500 channels in the near future. This is accomplished by use of high-powered transponder equipment (a radio or radar transceiver that automatically transmits a reply on reception of a certain signal) and digital compression that packs more channels into available bandwidth. The new satellite system has become one of the best-received and fastest-selling products in television and video technology.

"We envision the DSS system becoming part of an interactive 'digital TV center' that will be as easy to use as today's television sets," says Joseph P. Clayton, a Thomson executive vice president. "The receiver/decoder is typical of a first-generation digital interface for tomorrow's home entertainment center."

A competing new satellite system, PrimeStar, offers a receiving dish 36 to 39 inches in diameter that pulls in about 70 channels. Instead of selling its equipment to customers, PrimeStar leases it for about $8 a month. It is targeted primarily at households that do not have access to cable television. As of January 1995, about 100,000 households subscribed to PrimeStar.

Of the two satellite systems, only DDS is compatible with the high-definition television technology under development. Even so,

Satellite owners enjoy 150 channels of TV viewing in laser-disk sharpness and CD-quality sound.
(Photo courtesy RCA)

present TV sets will have to be replaced in order to take advantage of HDTV's greater resolution.

The digital high-definition television (HDTV) system was proposed by General Instrument in June 1990. In June 1993, HDTV competitors agreed to create a single system for the U.S. However, because of the cost and time involved in developing the technology, it may be another five to ten years before consumers will be able to buy HDTV sets, and the price tag could be about $10,000. Meanwhile, TV manufacturers are introducing bigger screen and wider screen sets that show movies in their original rectangular, theater-screen ratio, called "letterbox."

> The new satellite system has become one of the best-received and fastest-selling products in television and video technology.

Coming along much faster than high-definition television is interactive TV. Several major telephone, movie production, and cable television companies are forming partnerships and investing billions of dollars in the future of interactive TV. The technology enables viewers to have some interplay with what their TV receives, such as giving it home shopping commands, playing games on devices hooked up to the TV, or using the TV in combination with personal computers.

In 1994, Bell Atlantic, an East Coast group of telephone companies, became the first phone company to win approval from the Federal Communications Commission (FCC) to offer interactive TV. Some 38,000 homes in Toms River, New Jersey, were wired for interactive TV services on about 80 channels at prices less than comparable cable charges.

Meanwhile, dozens of other interactive TV projects involving television and telephone companies and, in some 18 cases, computer software companies, are either already under way or are in the planning stages. In California, Pacific Telesis, a major group of telephone companies, is building a $16-billion system that would wire the entire state for interactive TV by the year 2005. In Maryland,

Southwestern Bell telephone is preparing to offer phone services over a cable TV system it owns in Montgomery County. Subscribers will be able to buy cable and phone services and advanced phone features such as voice mail and caller-ID. Still in its infancy stages is technology to perfect "phonevision," where telephone users could see each other on miniature TV screens attached to their telephones.

The Walt Disney Company, one of the major producers of movie, television, and cable entertainment, entered the interactive TV race in mid-1994 when it announced plans to develop interactive projects with Ameritech Corporation and two regional telephone companies, Bell South and Southwestern Bell. The $4.4 billion joint venture would offer television viewers services over their telephone lines, including interactive home shopping, educational programs, games, movies-on-demand, travel assistance, and an advanced program selection system in addition to broadcast television and satellite network transmissions.

"Our goal is to use technological breakthroughs and new entertainment delivery systems to provide TV customers with a compelling and creative array of programming," says Michael Eisner, Disney's chief executive officer.

"The objective of this venture is to provide consumers with the choice they demand and deserve in video services," echoes Richard C. Notebaert, Ameritech's chief executive officer. "Our work with Disney would be designed to make cruising the information highway as fun and easy for our customers as it is useful for them."

Interactive television is a multibillion-dollar gamble for those envisioning vast profits from the technology. The big question is, if they build it, will anyone want it? Or, as John Tierney, *New York Times* media writer, put it: "Is the world ready for the empowered couch potato?"

"Television viewers keep hearing that they're about to merge into a global computerized information network, one grand Communicopia," says Tierney. "It will supposedly enable them to watch 500 channels, browse in electronic shopping malls and libraries, send a fax to Mount Everest, and maybe even learn to use the phrase 'digital interactive multimedia' in a sentence. The vision of a data highway into every living room is still based mainly on faith: If you build it, they will interact."

A *New York Times*/CBS News Poll indicates that most Americans are willing to pay a reasonable fee in order to control what is on their television screens.

The first commercially successful experiment of interactive television was started four years ago by Videoway in Montreal, Canada. Viewers pay $6.50 a month to use remote control pads that allow them to play along with the popular game show "Jeopardy!", or play video chess on their TV screen. They also can choose which camera angles to watch during baseball games, order instant replays during sports events, pick which segments to watch on news shows, calculate their income tax, scan classified ads and movie listings at local theaters, and even choose which commercials to watch.

> "The vision of a data highway into every living room is still based mainly on faith: If you build it, they will interact."

A survey indicates that the average Videoway subscriber uses the interactive TV system 8.5 hours a week. Three hours go to video games such as "Jeopardy!", and the remaining time is spent on data services, the most popular of which are weather reports, horoscopes, and lottery information. Subscribers reduced the amount of time spent watching regular television programming by about six hours a week, or about 20 percent. They use that time, plus a few added hours, on Videoway.

"The system is not creating a great impact or change, but it's developing new habits," says Andre H. Caron, director of the University of Montreal's New Technologies Research Laboratory. "With Videoway, people are learning to expect more and more from television."

What cable television executives find most remarkable about Videoway is that so many people are willing to pay for it. In Montreal, it reaches 160,000 households, that is, a quarter of the cable subscribers who are eligible to take the service.

Developers of the Canadian interactive TV system found that the public does not want a computer keyboard in their living room, and does prefer a familiar remote-control pad used to select choices on the television screen. Pushing a button causes a small receiving box on top the TV set to either download data, like a video game, or switch to another channel showing a different version of a TV program. Subscribers say they feel their TV set acts both as a computer and a Nintendo player. Viewers agree: "You watch TV in a different way." In America, viewers are interacting with their television sets by subscribing to the Interactive Network. For $20 a month, cable customers can interact with several popular television game shows, including "Jeopardy!" and "Wheel of Fortune." With "Jeopardy!", players choose the right question from a list of four possibilities that appear on the screen. During sporting events, players can make a play call and lock in their choice before the play develops on their TV screen. They can also record their guess of who the murderer is each week on "Murder, She Wrote" before the sleuth tells them who it is.

Computer users are already familiar with interactive systems such as CompuServe and America Online. They can browse through libraries, hold conferences, and play games with partners across the country via networking for about $10 a month. Their commands are sent out over telephone lines to a central computer at a company's headquarters.

In a survey of 3,500 CompuServe subscribers, more than 90 percent said they are "somewhat" to "very" interested in buying an interactive TV if it can help them make video telephone calls.

"We think the on-line participants represent the earliest adopters of technology," says Arnie Semsky, of the BBDO advertising agency in New York City. "We are eager to hear what they think about where the information highway is headed, especially in interactive TV."

Major players in the entertainment and communications industries began conducting field tests in 1994 to help determine whether the future of interactive services will show up on the television screen or on the computer monitor. These companies include Ameritech in Chicago; Bell Atlantic in Alexandria, Virginia; SNET in Hartford, Connecticut; Cox Cable in Omaha, Nebraska; TCI in Denver, Colorado; and Viacom in Castro Valley, California.

One of the biggest and most expensive tests so far of interactive television began in Orlando, Florida on December 14, 1994, with Time Warner Cable's five-year, $5-billion interactive venture, the Full Service Network. Heralded by its investors as "a turning point for the communications industry," viewers are offered new movies on demand, which can be taped by their VCRs, and services including home shopping, video games, news-on-demand, music, educational and sports programming. Also available are services where subscribers can order tickets to live sporting or entertainment events or peruse area restaurant menus. This test should prove how interested Americans are in interactive television and how much they are willing to pay for it.

For now, however, the *New York Times*/CBS News Poll indicated that most Americans would like to interact more with their televisions, and on average they would be willing to pay about $10 a month for a package of new features. The most popular feature would be the ability to order reruns of television programs.

Younger adults seem most enthusiastic about interactive television. Of respondents 18 to 29 years old, 82 percent are very interested in at least one interactive feature, and nearly half are willing to pay more than $15 a month for new features. (People younger than 18 were not surveyed.)

"The poll is evidence of a significant shift in people's attitudes toward television," says Steve Reynolds, who analyzes interactive media at LINK Resources. "Ten years ago, it was hard for people to even imagine using their televisions to choose camera angles or order products. But now they're willing to accept interactivity and pay a fairly realistic price for it. There's been a big change in expectations and in the way people watch television, especially among younger viewers and male viewers."

3-D TV

Three-dimensional television for consumers is still some years in the future, although technicians have already invented pioneering systems for depth-viewing.

A leader in this exciting technology is the 3D TV Corporation of San Rafael, California, which has created several universal interfaces for three-dimensional viewing on television sets as well as with computer and video game players. The interfaces drive the company's LCD (liquid crystal display) stereo eyeglasses and several models of Stereo-Visors, or LCD viewing eyeglasses, which are used with either computers or television sets. Eyeglasses range in cost from $150 to $350, and interfaces and other supporting equipment run from hundreds to thousands of dollars.

One thing is certain: Television is changing. More channels to watch, better pictures and sound from satellites or high-definition technology, bigger and wider screens, and some types of interactivity are going to be in television's—and the viewers'—future.

3

VCRs and Videotapes

The video recording era began in 1975 when the Sony Corporation introduced Betamax, the first videocassette recorder (VCR) for home use. Three years later, RCA introduced a second type of VCR—the VHS, or Video Home System, format. Since the two formats were not compatible and tapes on one machine would not record or play-back on the other, consumers had a choice to make; they decided they preferred the less expensive VHS system, and it soon dominated the market.

Major refinements to the VCR began to follow quickly. Akai brought out the first VCR with stereo sound and Dolby noise reduction, in 1981. JVC produced the first hi-fi VCR in 1983, and the first Super VHS machine four years later.

VCRs have become one of the most popular products of entertainment technology. As of January 1995, there were about 114 million VCRs in U.S. households, according to Electronic Industries Association figures. Many homes have more than one machine.

According to a Times Mirror study, VCRs tend to be used most often as videocassette players, rather than recorders, possibly because many people do not know how to use them to record programs.

Some 43 percent of those surveyed said they play videos "often," and 35 said they do so "sometimes." Only 20 percent of those surveyed said they use their VCR often to record TV programs. Only 23 percent said they often use the timer to record TV programs for later viewing, and 26 percent sometimes do this.

Some 36 percent of those surveyed reported using the VCR often to play rented or purchased tapes, mostly of movies. Americans spent $12 billion renting videocassettes in 1993. Movie studios report they now earn twice as much revenue from their movies when rented or sold as videocassettes for home viewing than they do from movie theater showings alone.

The first video rental store franchise, George Atkinson's Video Station, opened in 1978. A few years ago, there were about 30,000 independents in the U.S. Today there are only about 25,000 independents, because of competition from supermarkets that sell and/or rent movies on videotape and chain stores such as Blockbuster.

The first camcorder, a camera and video recorder in one unit, was introduced by Sony in 1983 with its BMC-110 BetaMovie. It weighed 6 pounds and recorded, but could not play back pictures taken with it. VHS-format camcorders soon followed, and then 8mm and VHS-C models. New technology enabled manufacturers to introduce lighter-weight models with many more features, such as the zoom lens, electronic view-finder, automatic focus, and built-in microphone.

Hitachi has demonstrated a tiny, digital camcorder that can shoot color video using a memory storage chip instead of tape. A production model of the solid-state camcorder could be ready by 1999. It would use a 400-megabyte flash memory chip the size of a sugar cube to record 30 minutes of video at less than VHS quality. Because the camcorder has no moving parts, it weighs only 20 ounces.

High-definition televisions, laser disk players, and camcorders are still years away, but HD video recorders can be purchased. However, they cost about $10,000, and while they can play VHS and Super-VHS tapes, they can't record a TV show or movie because they can only receive the MUSE analog signal, which is being broadcast only in Japan. So for all practical purposes, HD VCRs for use in America are not yet available.

A consortium of manufacturers and laboratories is working together to put the finishing touches on a high-definition television system. At the same time, many companies are working to define the standards that will dictate the way HDTV videos will be recorded and played.

Fifty companies that make up the Digital VCR Conference have settled on a digital VCR design that calls for a larger tape than standard VCRs use. These new tapes measure 4.9 × 3 × 0.57 inches and record 4½ hours at standard TV quality and 2¼ hours of high-definition TV. Smaller tape, for camcorder use, measures 2.6 × 1.9 × .48 inches and will record one hour of standard TV and one half hour of HDTV. Panasonic offers a professional model HD VCR, but consumer models, from Philips/Magnavox, may not be available for another year.

Meanwhile, a British company has invented a device that lets television viewers record two programs simultaneously on the same videotape. Japanese companies are showing interest in the device, which is a spin-off of research into technology to make three-dimensional films, according to Jack Ezra, founder of 3D Video Plus.

Just as consumers began to get used to hearing about high-definition and digital enhancements coming to new videocassette recorders, another technology threatens to perhaps make VCRs obsolete. Two groups of manufacturers are poised to offer the compact digital video disk or DVD, 5-inch versions of laser disks that will contain an entire movie in laserlike sharpness and CD-quality sound.

There are problems, however. DVD disks won't play on a computer but on a special new DVD player that could initially cost about $500. Disks would cost about $20 each. Also, the two competing DVD systems being developed are not compatible. The system designed by Sony and Philips will hold 135 minutes of digital video on a 5-inch CD, and a competing system developed by

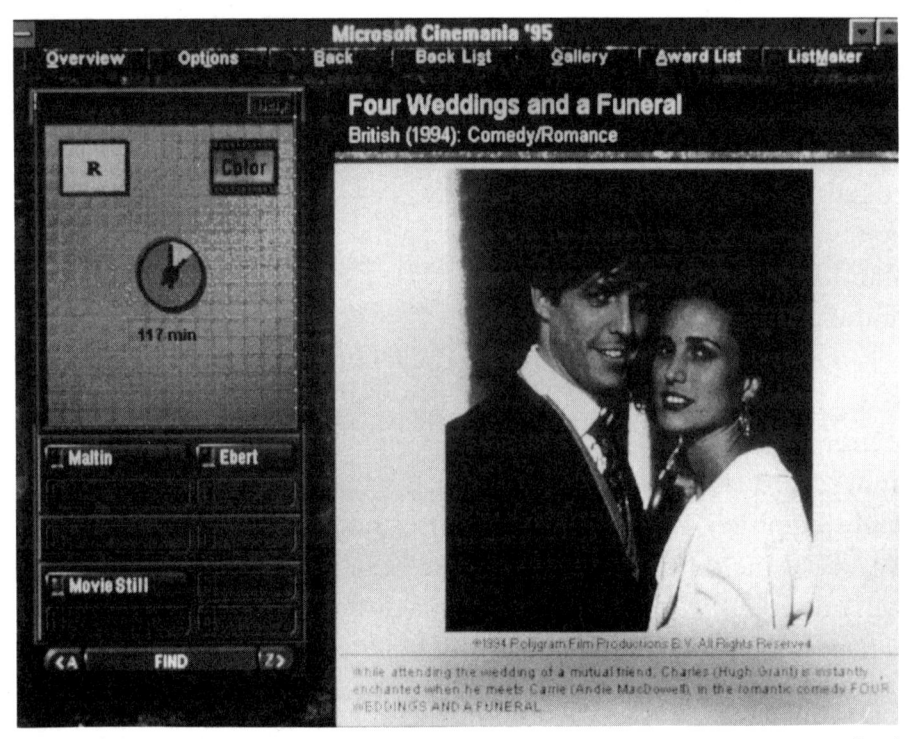

Movie information is available on computer disks, and full-length movies are soon to be stored on CD-size digital disks. (Photo courtesy Microsoft)

Toshiba, Time Warner, and Pioneer would hold even more data, perhaps storing as many as three movies on a single disk, in layers. Industry watchers envisioned a format war similar to the Betamax-VHS battle, but plans to merge the system were announced late in 1995.

Backers of both systems predict the DVD will eventually replace the VCR and movies on videocassette. Others, however, doubt that the public will be willing to embrace the new technology, since they have come to like using their VCRs so much. Many people also have invested in large videotape home libraries, which would keep them using the familiar VCR technology.

Meanwhile, another step into the future for video recording is a movement toward offering "movies on demand," via the home computer. Imagine it's raining or snowing out or maybe you hate to spend time picking up and returning videotapes at your local video rental store. Instead of going to the store, you could sit at your computer and ask a central video bank for a movie it has stored as a digital file on a computer called a video server. The movie would then be downloaded onto your computer for viewing on the monitor or, by connecting cables, to your television set. Newer and more frequently requested movies would be stored in the video bank computer's main memory, and older, less-watched movies stored on digital cassette tapes in a video archive. Thousands of viewers could have simultaneous access to the same video "file."

> Backers of both systems predict the DVD will eventually replace the VCR and movies on videocassette.

Microsoft Corporation of Redmond, Washington, a leader in computer software manufacturing, took the lead in providing movies-on-demand in May, 1994, by introducing its new "Tiger" software. This software can provide media-on-demand for services ranging from one small computer supplying movies to hotel guests to a more powerful machine satisfying the needs of several hundred corporate users. It also can supply tens of thousands of movie titles to hundreds of thousands of cable television customers. Field test trials are currently being conducted in the Seattle area. Another pay-per-view venture into movies and multimedia services on-demand was begun early in 1994 by the Oracle Corporation of Redwood City, California.

Perhaps more exciting than any of these ventures is the imminent arrival of the 6mm videocassette. Video industry sources predict the new tape, slightly smaller than the traditional 8mm tape now used in video recording, will be the way future cassettes will be recorded. It will employ new digital recording technology that promises a crystal clear picture and better sound than present video- tape offers.

Americans have come to love their VCRs, and high-definition and digital improvements are bound to make us love them even more. Movies-on-demand, by way of our computer, can only add to our VCR enjoyment. Many people may prefer watching movies on 5-inch CDs, but it is doubtful that VCRs will fade from the home entertainment scene anytime soon. They will only get better.

4

Video Games Tekkies Play

Video games have become one of the most exciting forms of entertainment since Magnavox introduced Odyssey, the first home video game, in 1972. Odyssey was originally a simplistic tennis game, but later versions offered hockey, handball, basketball, and other games.

Odyssey and several competing video game formats began to fade from popularity in 1977 when Atari introduced its 800 Video Computer System, which used interchangeable game cartridges. While the games were fun to play, the graphics and sound were of poor quality. Home video game players who wanted to play arcade-quality games bought a personal computer such as the Commodore 64 that offered more advanced computer-driven game software.

Nintendo, one of the leading video game companies, changed the home arcade picture in 1986 when it introduced Super Mario Brothers, the first game for its 8-bit Nintendo Entertainment System (NES). Each cartridge offered improved visuals and sound for better arcade-quality play. Competition soon emerged from other manufacturers such as Sega and NEC, which offered 16-bit machines with even better graphics and other enhancements, starting a battle for supremacy in the home video game industry that continues to this day.

Some of the newest video games are played on Sega Genesis' CDX Multimedia CD-ROM player.
(Photo courtesy Sega)

About a third of American households now own at least one of several types of video game systems currently on the market. Sales of game software have soared to more than $6 billion a year, and players spend another $1.5 billion renting video games.

A 1994 Times Mirror survey reported that, as expected, households with younger children were far more likely to own a video game system than were others. Some 68 percent of those surveyed who had children living in the home said they had a video game system, compared to only 9 percent of those aged 65 or older. However, one fifth of all video game players are in households without children, and half of all Sega Genesis owners are older than 18.

In households with a video game system, 12 percent of those surveyed reported playing with the game "often," while 17 percent said they did so "sometimes." Twenty-seven percent of those surveyed aged 18 to 29 said they played with a home system "sometimes" or "often."

Sega's 32-bit action game, Midnight Raiders, incorporates live video action with animation.
(Photo courtesy Sega)

Adults often feel their children leave them in the dust when it comes to playing video games. "My son, now 12, has been trouncing me at video games since he was five years old," admits David Sheff, author of *Video Games: A Guide for Savvy Parents*, writing in *TV Guide*. "Over that time I have watched the games become a national obsession—nine out of ten children play, and many of them play for hours a day."

"Parents continue to spend more and more money on games featuring clever characters such as Sonic the Hedgehog or Super Mario, and downright unsavory ones such as Kano. Kano is the mercenary/extortionist/thief in 'Mortal Kombat' who beats up his

> "The games [have] become a national obsession—nine out of ten children play, and many of them play for hours a day."

adversaries and finishes them off by pulling out their still-beating hearts. Fun guys like that."

Sheff has written two books about the social, educational, and psychological effects of video games and derived some significant conclusions. For example, young people who play video games too much may not do as well in school as those who play them in moderation, but video game-playing can supplement learning at school and it may even be good for players.

Game-playing can be especially helpful to young people who have problems with attentiveness or self-esteem. Some games encourage reading, whether through on-screen instructions, manuals, or video game magazines.

No video game player's library is complete without the megahit Mighty Morphin Power Rangers. (Photo courtesy Sega)

28 ENTERTAINMENT

Steven Silvern, professor of early childhood education at Auburn University in Auburn, Alabama, says games "permit the practice of skills not often incorporated into the school curriculum." For example, sports games such as the John Madden football series or NBA Jam help young players learn to become strategists. Puzzle or maze-based games such as Gear Works, Barney's Hide and Seek, and Tetris 2 require problem-solving and other cognitive skills. Role-playing, fantasy, and strategy games such as Illusion of Gaia and The Secret of Monkey Island encourage young imaginations.

> Games "permit the practice of skills not often incorporated into the school curriculum."

Computer games that have been adapted for cartridge systems expose young players to such diverse topics as geography (such as Where in the World is Carmen Sandiego?), history, politics, and even resource management and the environment, as seen in SimCity 2000.

"But it's all in what a parent or young person chooses," says David Sheff. "While certain games encourage reading and thinking, others teach much more violent skills—from punching and kicking to burning and decapitating. The industry's new ratings system helps you weed these out."

In response to parental concerns, two competing interactive software rating systems were designed in 1994. Most video game makers have adopted movie-type ratings developed by the Interactive Digital Software Association, and more than 250 game titles have been rated. Ratings caution what game contents are for "early childhood" (nothing parents would find inappropriate for ages 3 to 6), "kids" (minimal violence for ages 6 to 13), "teens" (some strong language and/or suggestive themes, for ages 13 to 16), and "mature" (some intense violence, stronger language, and mature sexual themes, for ages 17 or older). An "Adults Only" rating may include more graphic sexual content and/or violence. Only two titles have received this rating so far.

One inadvertent control over games too violent or sexual for younger players is their price tag. Since video games cost $60 on average, younger players usually have to ask their parents to buy the title they want.

Avid young video game players prefer their games on the action and violent side. The game maker Acclaim sold $50 million worth of Mortal Kombat II in its first week in stores. A notice on the box cautions that the game may not be appropriate for players under 17.

Does video game playing turn young players into antisocial nerds? "No," says Sheff. "Not if they play together." When groups of young people play video games, they become animated and excited, which is good." His research also has found that "in reasonable doses," video games can be a social benefit, even bringing families together.

Experts say the violence in many video games may be harmful to younger players. "Video games provide young people with a strong sense of dramatic victory without the slightest bit of physical danger," says Brian Stonehill, director of media studies at Pomona College, Pomona, California. "Most players over five or six know the difference between game violence and real life. But too much time with the ultraviolent games can have harmful effects, especially for younger players."

Taking a stronger view against violence on video games is Parker Page, a psychologist who founded the Children's Television Resource and Education Center in Washington, D.C. "Video games can put children at risk," he maintains. "It makes them more aggressive, at least for the short term, and more tolerant of aggression."

Video game-playing undoubtedly can help young people become more comfortable and expert with computers and other technology. However, most video games are designed for and played by boys. Some 82 percent of those who play games on the Super Nintendo Entertainment System are boys. This means that most young girls are excluded from an experience that can help them appreciate and be comfortable with technology.

A study by University of Miami professor of education Eugene Provenzo, Jr. noted that a majority of girls who were asked about video games said they did not like them because there were no positive characters to which they could relate. Maybe video game creators need to develop software that's more relevant to girls.

The same technology that may allow renters of movies on videocassettes to order titles via their home computer is also likely to enable video game players to rent games without going to the store. Major video game makers such as Sega and Newleaf Entertainment have joined with Blockbuster Video stores to test-market the new electronic delivery system.

Video game software could also be stored electronically at rental stores and downloaded on demand onto specially-designed reprogrammable video game cartridges. These cartridges look and play just like a standard video game cartridge and can be reprogrammed an unlimited number of times, allowing retailers to customize their inventory of rental titles to match consumer demand.

How about playing video games over your television set from cable TV? Acclaim Entertainment has invested $85 million in a venture with Tele-Communications Inc. (TCI) to transmit Mortal Kombat and other games into players' homes by way of cable TV wires.

Perhaps the hottest thing to happen to video games since Donkey Kong is the anticipated start of The Sega Channel, a cable and satellite television channel devoted exclusively to playing Sega video games. It is a joint venture of Sega, TCI, and Time Warner. For about $15 a month, viewers can select from a menu of about 50 Sega games and download a title for play on their Sega Genesis player. Also, new games for use on interactive TV networks telecast by cable and satellite might have as many as 1,000 players at once.

This brings up a whole new video game in town, and it's called interactive. Some of the new games for this "player in command" technology will be in the traditional 16-bit format, programmed to play on existing game players. The best of the new games, however, will require purchasing either add-on technology or new machines capable of playing video games in the powerful new 32- and 64-bit systems. Interactive video games are the subject of the next chapter in this tour of electronic entertainment.

5

Multimedia and Interactive Technology

Multimedia and interactive technologies—two of the driving forces of the new information revolution—enable users to personalize their high-tech learning or entertainment experiences.

Multimedia refers to electronic hardware and software products that use various media such as text, graphics, animation, and audio to deliver information. The newest of the machines—from computers with built-in CD-ROM drives to video game players—also are interactive. This feature allows the user to pick and choose from a variety of information options so that he or she has a say in how to use the technology.

"In the digital world, the word 'media,' which once implied 'one-way,' suggests interactive, individualized, seeking one's own level," says Nicholas Negroponte, director of The Media Laboratory at Massachusetts Institute of Technology, in *Modern Maturity* in 1994. "Computers [processing digitized multimedia information] can help us decide what we want to see, hear, or read. They can edit, expand, and personalize information. They let us interact with it."

Negroponte predicts a future where when you wake up in the morning, you will have a section of the electronic newspaper called "The Daily Me," devoted to people, places, and ideas that interest you. When you turn on the car radio, it will automatically play news important to you. When you want to look at a movie, the system will recommend an excellent one to interest you. While this may sound like an electronic ego trip, Negroponte predicts that personalization, through multimedia, will be a valuable addition to our lives.

To utilize the best of the new multimedia software, a fairly powerful computer is needed, with at least 8 megabytes of random access memory (RAM). It also should be equipped with a CD-ROM drive and a sound card that adds music to games and other software. Another route to multimedia is through a stand-alone system designed to be connected to a TV set.

Video game players like their action superfast and graphics that are so lifelike they look three-dimensional. They also like to take control of the game they are playing, to move the hero into action scenes they want him to enter next.

Multimedia and interactive equipment includes TV sets, computers, camcorders, laser disk, and other players. (Photo courtesy I.B.M.)

Interactive features are incorporated in many new CD-ROM computer disks, for entertainment or education. (Photo courtesy I.B.M.)

In order to fill such a hefty bill, computer and game makers are upgrading both hardware and software or are inventing new machines that will allow interaction. Millions of dollars are being spent to develop and manufacture 32- and 64-bit systems that will be faster and can hold more memory than the standard 16-bit players now available.

Yet, present 16-bit players are no slouches in the games they can play. Both Sega and Nintendo have 16-bit machines as well as more powerful players pitched as "entertainment systems" that sell for about $300. Meanwhile, competition is growing from makers of multimedia computers with built-in CD-ROM drives that play the latest interactive games and educational disks.

Some of the most popular computer games are from George Lucas, creator of the *Star Wars* movies. His best-selling interactive LucasArts games include X-Wing, a computer-driven space combat continuance of the starfighter adventures of Luke Skywalker against the Dark Forces of the Empire. Taking advantage of the latest in game technology, it offers lifelike sound such as laser blasts and fiery explosions, aerial hit-and-run raids and dogfights, over 50 deep space and Death Star surface missions, advanced camera replay, dialogue and music sound tracks direct from the Star Wars movies, and digitized movie sound effects such as the roar of the Imperial TIE fighters. Other popular LucasArts CD adventures are TIE Fighter and Rebel Assault.

At present, there are at least seven different interactive systems on the market that all make use of CD-ROM (Compact Disk-Read Only Memory) technology. While similar in appearance to CD audio disks, they contain digitized computer data like that found on a floppy diskette or hard disk drive instead of containing digitized music. A CD-ROM can store up to 650 megabytes of data (or about

LucasArts introduced its first space combat simulator with X-Wing, an interactive video game inspired by the *Star Wars* movies.
(Photo courtesy LucasArts)

MULTIMEDIA AND INTERACTIVE TECHNOLOGY 35

500 floppy disks worth of data), on a compact disk, enough storage space for a complete set of encyclopedias or a phone book containing listings for the entire country.

Currently, there are two categories of CD-ROMs available: CD-ROM drives that are connected to personal computers, and stand-alone players that are self-contained and designed to be connected to television home entertainment systems.

Pioneer's Laser Active Multi-Format Player offers games, movies, music, education, and "how-to" software, and is compatible with the existing movie, music, and game software already in millions of homes. It has the capacity to play all sizes of conventional compact disks, CD-videos, and laser disks, delivering high quality images and impressive high-fidelity sound. It sells for about $720. Also available are three optional control-packs: one compatible with Sega Genesis cartridges and Sega CDs; another

X-Wing takes game users into a Rebel Alliance space adventure to destroy Darth Vader's Imperial Forces.
(Photo courtesy LucasArts)

Three models of 3DO interactive multiplayer systems. (Photo courtesy 3DO Company)

developed in cooperation with NES's TurboGrafx-CD game player; and a third pack providing compatibility with LaserKaraoke music disks. Each costs about $480.

The 3DO Company of Redwood City, California, is developing technologies for interactive entertainment with a worldwide standard in mind. Backed by Matsushita, Time Warner, and AT&T, its product, called an Interactive Multiplayer, offers amazing speed and superior graphics. Featuring "full digital synergy," the system plays standard music CDs, allows viewing family photos on CDs, and has interactive CD software for entertainment, education, and information. Because the system uses compact disks instead of cartridges, the sound quality is excellent. A 3DO system, made by GoldStar and Panasonic, costs about $400 and includes two game titles. Also available is the company's M2 Accelerator, a peripheral upgrade that provides faster game play. 3DO also can be played on computers with a plug-in board.

By licensing its technology to hardware and software companies such as Panasonic and MCA, 3DO is able to take full advantage of its ties to Hollywood and the entertainment industry, one of the keys to the format's future success. CDs used to launch 3DO, for example, were based on Stephen Spielberg's hit movie *Jurassic Park*.

3DO players offer the lastest technology in video games, such as Samurai Showdown by Crystal Dynamics. (Photo courtesy 3DO Company)

Scenes specifically used in production of the game were filmed on location during the shooting of the movie.

Coming soon from 3DO is a 64-bit higher-powered add-on, to play CD movies. Game titles that can be played on 3DO machines include Panasonic's Super Street Fighter II Turbo, EA's Road Rash, Crystal Dynamics' Gex, Universal's Demolition Man, and EA Sports' FIFA International Soccer, which has been called the most realistic-looking sports game available. The games cost from $30 to $70.

Philips Consumer Electronics' Interactive Compact Disk System, called CD-i, comes in either a basic model for $300 or one equipped with a digital video cartridge for faster game play and full motion video, at a cost of $500. The company considers CD-i a complete home entertainment system, not just a game player, because it also plays movies and music. The CD-i machine enables owners to watch movies on a 5-inch disk, a format that is expected to become very popular and could eventually rival videocassettetapes.

Also capable of playing 3- and 5-inch audio compact disks and CD-videos, the Philips interactive unit can store and project photographic images from 35mm film on special photo CDs. Adding a special cartridge, it also will play laser disks with their great clarity and sound. The player costs about $700.

The CD system of Sega of America, based in Redwood City, California, is designed to be compatible with the current Sega Genesis systems. Its CD-ROM games offer hundreds of high quality graphic screens and CD quality audio for special effects and background music. It also plays audio CDs.

The partnership of Sega of America and Sony Imagesoft allows for the production of games based on popular movies such as *Dracula* and *Hook*. With the use of digitized film of real action sequences, there are great possibilities for software with movie-like images. The Sega-Sony multimedia entertainment system, selling for about $300, will merge movies, music, and video games into one interactive

Many museums invite visitors to take part in interactive TV and video services. (Photo courtesy I.B.M.)

venture, offering games on home players that are of the quality of those available now only in arcades. Sega's newest technology is a 32X hardware upgrade for the Sega Genesis, for $150.

Super Nintendo, a system priced at about $100, is capable of playing a library of 500 games, including Tin Star, Super Punch-Out, and Super Mario Paint, for $30 to $80. A Super Game Boy attachment for $60 lets users play Game Boy games in color. Nintendo's latest offering is the 64-bit Ultra 64 system, for $250, for playing three-dimensional video games on a TV screen.

Another video game maker, Atari, offers the Atari Jaguar player for about $250 and games such as Alien vs. Predator and Doom for $60 to $70. A CD attachment is available for about $200.

JVC's X'EYE system, for about $400, plays Sega CD and Genesis games and other types of interactive compact disks.

Sony's PlayStation, a 32-bit system soon to be introduced,

Video arcades offer customers multimedia and interactive experiences.
(Photo courtesy I.B.M.)

will cost about $410. The design of the PlayStation shows the growing impact of the newest generation of semiconductor logic, a manufacturing process where wires are shrunk to just half a micron wide. By comparison, a human hair is about 75 microns wide. The miniaturization enables designers to put entire databases onto a single silicon chip that has benefits in both cost and production methods.

The PlayStation processor will contain about one million transistors and be composed of a R3000 microprocessor, a graphics processor, and a special processor for decompressing stored graphical images. The PlayStation reportedly will be able to generate three-dimensional computer graphics superior to anything else on the market.

More of tomorrow's video game player and computer game technology was unveiled at the Consumer Electronics Show in Las Vegas, Nevada, in January, 1995. New video game machines from Nintendo, Sega, Sony, 3DO, and Atari are virtual computers with far more processing power than many of the current top personal computers using Intel's powerful Pentium chip. Instead of costing up to $3,000, as Pentium computers do, the game players will start at less than $500 and will probably sell for half that soon after.

Television "set-top computers" (small computers that are set atop the TV set) based on a new generation of media processor chips are about to be marketed. They will translate streams of digital information sent over cable or telephone networks to let viewers select movies when they want them. They also will offer computer animation capabilities rivaling the quality of home video game players.

Whatever format the video game player of tomorrow may be, the software is likely to reflect what attracts the players. If developers are looking for a model out of today's interactive game software to pattern future offerings, they might not look any further than Star Trek: The Next Generation Interactive Technical Manual. Available on CD-ROM for Macintosh and IBM Windows computers, it is amazing even to those who are not among the legions of "Star Trek" fans.

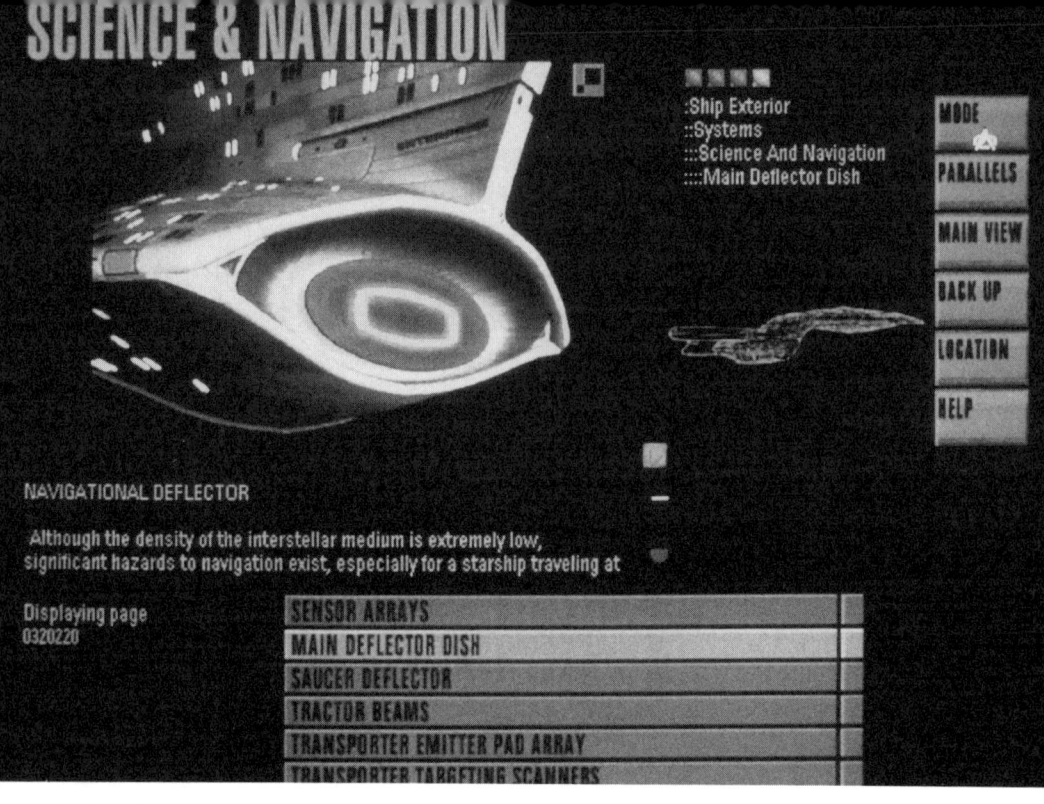

Star Trek: The Next Generation Interactive Technical Manual, a CD-ROM disk, simulates the experience of being onboard the USS *Enterprise.* (Photo courtesy Simon & Schuster Interactive)

The $70 disk virtually puts players on board for a day with Starfleet command. A walkthrough is conducted by voices of the television series' stars, and features new three-dimensional technology from Apple called QuickTime VR (for virtual reality). Viewers control pans and zooms of lifelike graphics or click on various control panels and gadgets to learn about the technologies and philosophies that drive the starship's crew. Reviewers call it "state-of-the-art" in interactive video game playing.

In fast pursuit of that disk is Wing Commander III: Heart of the Tiger, from Origin, the latest CD-ROM installment of the science-fiction action game series. Produced at a cost of more than $4 million, it stars Mark Hamill of *Star Wars.* Integrating over three hours of live-action video with futuristic sets and three-dimensional

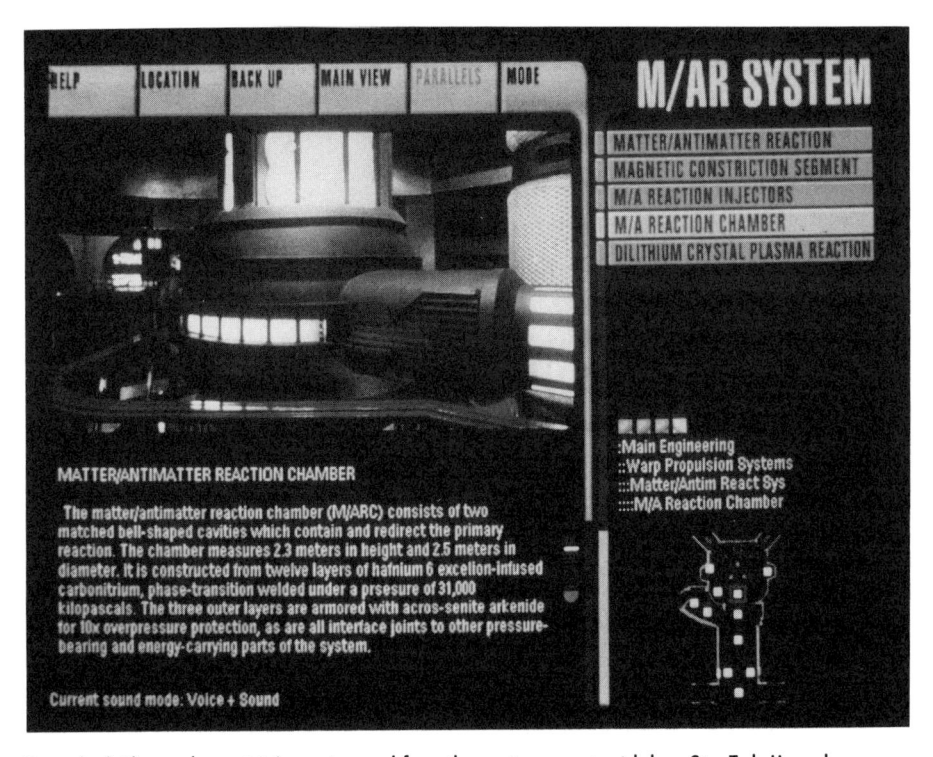

From the bridge to the captain's quarters and from the engine room to sick bay, Star Trek Manual users can zoom in or out of a scene, navigate from one room to another, and view objects from all angles.
(Photo courtesy Simon & Schuster Interactive)

space-flight simulation, it has been called the most advanced game disk yet by some critics.

Keeping up with the latest technology and models of computers and video game players that offer the most in multimedia and interactive features may be a little overwhelming, but the direction is clear. Competing manufacturers of both hardware and software are eager to take the lead in this very lucrative entertainment market. Those who offer the most in interactive games for the best price will be the winners.

6

Virtual Reality at the Movies

Only a few decades ago, watching a movie meant going to a darkened theater and seeing a film projected on a screen. That all changed when television began showing movies in the mid-1940s. The way movies are viewed changed again when videocassette recorders were introduced in 1975 and pre-recorded tapes of movies could be shown on TV sets. Now movies can be viewed on computers, from floppy disks, and CD-ROMs.

In the 1950s, movie producers and theater owners tried to stem the competition from television by making movies bigger and wider, through technology such as Cinerama and CinemaScope. Today, since more people rent movies on videotape than buy tickets to see movies in a theater, and competition from viewing movies on computers is growing, moviegoers are being drawn back into the theaters because of new technology that makes what is shown on the screen more real and exciting than ever.

The name of this movie game is virtual reality, and it is capturing the imagination of many thousands of moviegoers. Audiences are being swept into vast panoramas and headlong action on an outsize screen in a specially-built theater, or in a new concept in entertainment—a combination movie and theme park ride.

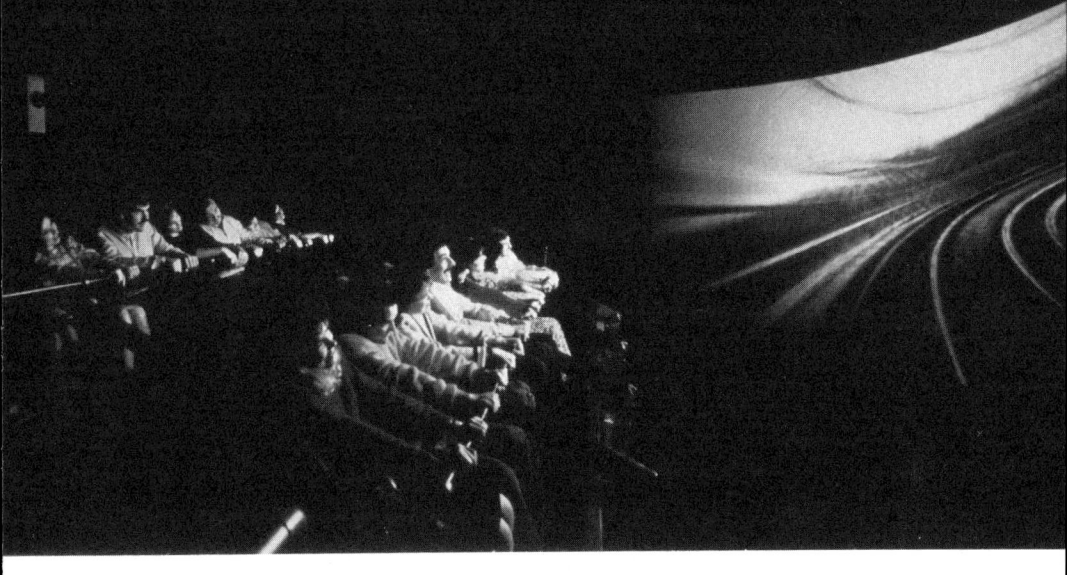

Simulated reality theaters like Showscan's take audiences on exciting virtual adventures.
(Photo courtesy Showscan Entertainment)

Three companies—Imax, Iwerks Entertainment, and Showscan—are competing in a battle of the big screens to create a future where their giant screens with simulations of real-life experiences (virtual reality) play a major role. Specially-built theaters, some at theme parks and others at major museums, show virtual reality movies on screens several stories high and as wide as 90 feet, with intensified picture clarity and sound.

Showscan, based in Culver City, California, added motion simulation in which movie theater seats tip sideways or up and down in synchronization with hair-raising swoops and turns. The technology virtually puts viewers into high-speed action sequences such as car races, downhill skiing, and outer-space exploration.

Iwerks, based in Burbank, California, opened the first in a chain of multi-attraction centers, Cinetropolis, a $15 million complex in Ledyard, Connecticut. It combines three attractions under one roof: a giant-screen theater, a 360-degree wraparound screen, and a motion simulator. Computer-controlled seats pitch and roll in unison with specially projected images to accompany attractions such as a filmed roller-coaster ride and a fantasy underwater chase.

Showscan, meanwhile, has opened a simulator theater at the Universal Citywalk in Los Angeles and plans another for Manhattan. Among the new attractions are a film ride that takes audiences on a careening, stomach-turning subterranean journey. A leader in the production and exhibition of exciting movie-based entertainment attractions shown in large-screen special-format theaters, Showscan has its virtual reality system in theaters located in theme parks, shopping centers, museums, and exposition centers around the world.

Imax, the oldest and most prominent giant-screen company, based in Toronto, Canada, also designs and supplies projection and sound systems and produces and distributes films for large-screen theaters. In 1994, it installed a futuristic theater within the nine-screen Sony multiplex center at Manhattan's Lincoln Square. The company also installed both the Naturemax Theater at the American Museum of Natural History in Manhattan and the domed Omni Theater at the Liberty Science Center in Jersey City, New Jersey.

> Movie industry sources say audiences want a more realistic experience when they go to a movie theater. "... What the public really wants is some experience that goes beyond the commonplace."

Inside the Sony Imax Theater in Manhattan, patrons find gift shops, black and gold palm trees, and nine ornate movie palaces seating a total of 3,600 moviegoers. Prime attractions of the multiplex are the 3-D Imax shows "Into the Deep" and "The Last Buffalo," seen on a movie screen 80 feet high and 100 feet wide. The three-dimensional movies are seen while wearing a special 3D headset, in oversized seats that rock with the action on-screen. Sony Dynamic Digital Sound adds to the experience of virtually being undersea or watching a buffalo stampede.

Movie industry sources say audiences want a more realistic experience when they go to a movie theater. "Seventy percent of U.S. box office ticket sales come from movies that are wide screen, stereo sound, with a lot of adventure and special effects," says Douglas Trumbull, inventor of the Showscan giant-screen process. "That indicates that what the public really wants is some experience that goes beyond the commonplace."

Trumbull compares his giant-screen film concepts to the highly sensory "space trip" sequences of the classic movie *2001: A Space Odyssey*, a film that he served as a visual effects supervisor. "It's time for a new kind of film industry to emerge," says Trumbull, "and it's going to emerge in a form that's probably closest to the Cinetropolis multi-attraction. We're going to see a completely different kind of viewing habitat. A more diverse but more powerful and immersive entertainment in an urban entertainment setting."

Not all the virtual reality in movies is experienced in theaters. Many video arcades are offering virtual reality that combines a movie with a video game.

Virtual World goes beyond the video arcade to become a digital theme park offering simulated interactive adventures. (Photo courtesy Virtual World)

Virtual World "factoids" contain bays and pods where game players interact with technology for virtual adventures. (Photo courtesy Virtual World)

Those who like their film adventures super high-tech get it at the Virtual World shop in the San Francisco suburb of Walnut Creek, called the world's first digital theme park. Seated in futuristic seats that look more like spaceships, movie time-travelers play a virtual reality movie-game called BattleTech. The 10-minute interactive video adventure takes viewer-riders down to a barren planet to neutralize a platoon of aggressive robots. Players or "pilots" are briefed in preparation for the journey ahead, then are taken to a variety of destinations. While on a virtual reality mission, they are free to move and interact with game characters and adventures. Afterward, pilots engage in a debriefing and receive a log as a permanent record of the adventure. Another virtual reality movie-game offered is "Red Planet," a Martian hovercraft race through the mines of Mars.

Other Virtual World "factoids" are in San Diego, Pasadena, Chicago, Houston, Las Vegas, Atlanta, and eight in Japan, with more to open in this country and around the world.

Sega, the video game maker, offers more virtual reality at its arcade in the Luxor hotel in Las Vegas, Nevada. Packed with the latest in video games, the arcade features Sega's R360, a fighter-plane simulator that straps customers into a semi-enclosed cockpit with an integral video

A pilot at the controls of his virtual reality pod, engaging in interaction between other players.
(Photo courtesy Virtual World)

> "With the advent of in-home entertainment, it's becoming more and more difficult to lure potential audiences out of their homes.'"

monitor. The virtual reality movie-game takes riders on an aeronautical shoot-'em-up in which they can move their cockpit seat as the spacecraft moves, recreating the dips and turns of an aerial space battle.

There is also Virtual Formula Racing, which comprises eight race car simulators, each facing a rear-projection monitor. Each racer sits in his or her own car and races against seven other players on a virtual course, feeling every bump, skid, and crash. The cars actually move around slightly as riders accelerate, steer, and collide.

"With the advent of in-home entertainment, it's becoming more and more difficult to lure potential audiences out of their homes," says Suzanne Zumbrunne, marketing coordinator of Showscan Entertainment. "However, Showscan delivers the kind of state-of-the-art excitement that today's audiences

Virtual World's Battle Tech puts video game players into the action. (Photo courtesy Virtual World)

are looking for. Our most important objective is to create the most thrilling motion picture experience in the world."

From these and other visual entertainment experiences around the country, virtual reality appears definitely to be going to the movies. Whether today's and certainly tomorrow's moviegoers watch movies at home, at video arcades, or in new giant and surround-screen theaters, it looks like they will become increasingly more a part of the movie they watch.

7

That's Edutainment!

As Mary Poppins sang, "A Spoonful of Sugar Makes the Medicine Go Down," edutainment (education + entertainment) is an increasingly popular way in which computer and game player software is making learning fun. Many of today's young computer whizzes got their start in the use of information technology by playing Broderbund's now-famous game, Where in the World Is Carmen Sandiego? While playing the international detective computer game they also learn some geography. A follow-up disk, Where In Space Is Carmen Sandiego? is an astronomy-oriented detective game offering great sound effects and breathtaking color images of the planets. An on-line database enables players to acquire valuable information about the solar system.

Broderbund, of Novato, California, stands out as a publisher of edutainment software because its products appeal to both the home and school markets because they are both fun and educational. Most of the programs come with idea-packed teachers' guides and special purchasing options for schools.

Another edutainment leader is EduQuest, an education division of IBM, located in Atlanta, Georgia. Among its most successful educational entertainment programs are Lessons from History: A Celebration of Blackness and The African American Experience: A History.

Thus far, most edutainment programs are aimed at pre-teenagers, but their value to young people should not be minimized.

"This new emphasis on home education can only be to our advantage," says Leslie Eiser, a teacher with degrees in both education and computer science, in *Technology & Learning* magazine. "There will be more software to choose from; creativity will increase; graphics and sound will improve by leaps and bounds (as competition increases); and prices will drop."

Some edutainment titles fit better into the school curriculum than others, such as the Carmen Sandiego series and another geography program, Software Toolworks' Mario Is Missing, and Davidson's science-oriented Zoo Keeper.

"Students may disagree on how compelling a particular storyline or game is," says Eiser. "Teachers may worry about how much time various programs spend on chases, searches, and other non-curricular elements. But overall, the best (edutainment) titles have a comfortable place in the classroom."

More difficult for teachers to fit into classroom study are puzzle or problem-solving edutainment games, such as Sierra On-Line's Castle of Dr. Brain and Binary Zoo's Mystery at the Museum. These games have players moving through adventure-filled environments, solving word and number puzzles, memory challenges, and a variety of other brain-teasers.

"The programs certainly qualify as edutainment, and at their best, challenge students to do some tough thinking," says Eiser. "To

> "This new emphasis on home education can only be to our advantage. There will be more software to choose from; creativity will increase; graphics and sound will improve by leaps and bounds (as competition increases); and prices will drop."

use them in the classroom, however, requires considerable flexibility. They have the most potential as enrichment activities or in the hands of a creative teacher who can engage teams of students in cooperative problem solving activities using the software as a springboard."

Something new that is aimed at teens and older players is Redshift, an interactive astronomy edutainment program from Maxis, of Orinda, California. The CD-ROM-based software was created by computer programmers and astronomers who had been members of the former Soviet Union's space program. The rocket scientists drew upon computer programs written for cosmonauts and data from the former Soviet Union's numerous space probes to create the realistic software.

Redshift holds data for 250,000 stars and 40,000 deep space objects such as radio stars, quasars, nebulae, and black holes. Utilizing a zoom feature, for example, users can move backward and forward in time to print out a picture of the sky as it appeared at the moment of their birth. Zooming outward, planets can be toured, along with all their moons, asteroids, and comets. Mars can be landed

Computer software is playing an increasingly important role in classroom education. (Photo courtesy I.B.M.)

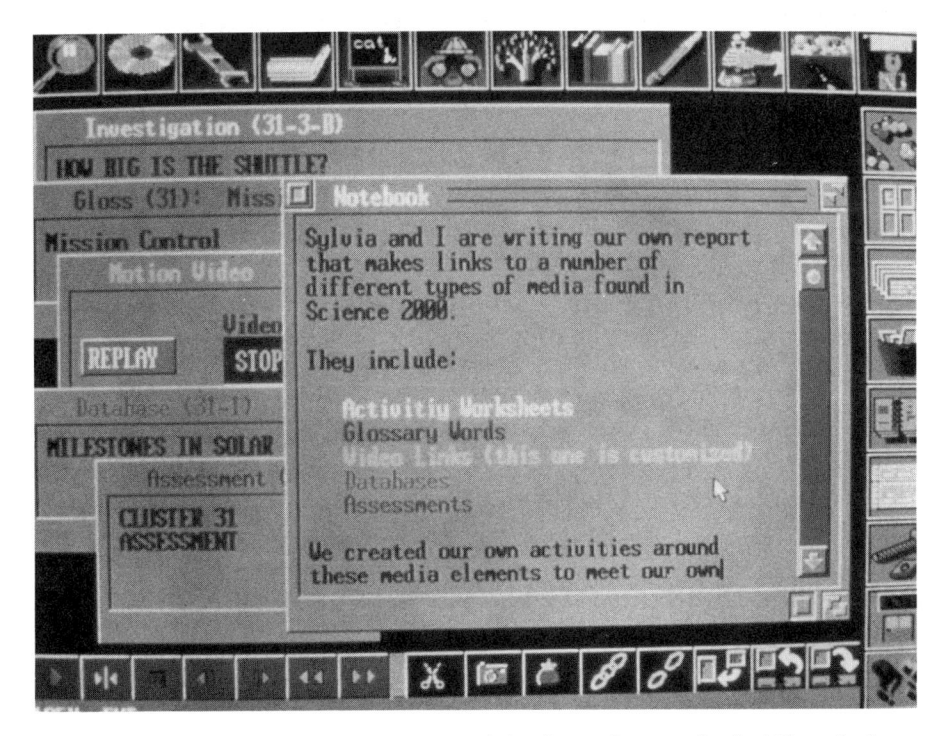

Reports written on a computer incorporate many research disciplines such as use of audio/video technology and database information searches. (Photo courtesy I.B.M.)

on and its canyons explored. Quicktime movies allow users to create stellar objects to observe, such as moons orbiting planets.

The full text of the *Penguin Astronomy Dictionary* is also included, along with more than 700 astronomical photographs and numerous film clips showing things like astronauts driving their Moon rover and the spacecraft *Viking* making a soft landing on the surface of Mars.

Many companies now produce educational software, though many emphasize drills and practice to complement the curricula they cover. "Maxis is markedly different because it deals in principles," says Doreen Nelson, professor of environmental design at California State Polytechnic at Pomona.

In Sim City, a Maxis game player is an urban planner of an imaginary city whose data is based on real-world information and statistics. Starting with an empty screen, the player builds a simulated

Communicating on-line over an Internet service, a user can access information almost instantly anywhere in the world. (Photo courtesy I.B.M.)

city by adding residential areas, police and fire departments, shopping areas, and businesses. From there, the player becomes involved in population, pollution, and tax problems. Questions, solutions, sacrifices and trade-offs result, challenging players to do some critical thinking.

"Players think there is an answer to every question, but the questions change over time," says Jeff Braun, founder of Maxis. "There's no win or lose playing Sim City, just cause and effect."

Sim Earth is an edutainment program focusing on environmental concerns. "It's amazing that a game company could put together so many concepts we use in science," says David Felt, a science teacher at Monterey (California) High School.

Also available for teens and adults are several science-oriented edutainment computer disks and CD-ROM programs from Knowledge Adventure of La Crescenta, California. Users put on three-dimensional glasses to view images that seem to pop out of the computer monitor. Bug Adventure takes viewers into the worlds of creepy, crawly things, while 3-D Body Adventure is a tour of the human body. Isaac Asimov's Science Adventure II includes movies, games, and simulated experiments. An exciting roller-coaster ride provides a demonstration of acceleration and speed.

"Knowledge Adventure's edutainment products encourage exploratory learning by tapping the innate sense of interest and curiosity that people of all ages have about things new and different," says the company's founder, Bill Gross. "Through sophisticated digital technology, we construct formal teaching methods and bring knowledge to life."

Gross boasts pioneering in several new technologies that provide users with unique experiences that support and enhance educational objectives. This includes compression technology that combines high-quality still images, full-motion video, simulations, digitized speech and music, stereo MIDI (Musical Instrument Digital Interface) music, sound and text on both floppy disks and CD-ROMs. The company also utilizes ZoomScape, an interactive movie technology that brings virtual

Educational software can combine science instruction with grammar lessons. (Photo courtesy I.B.M.)

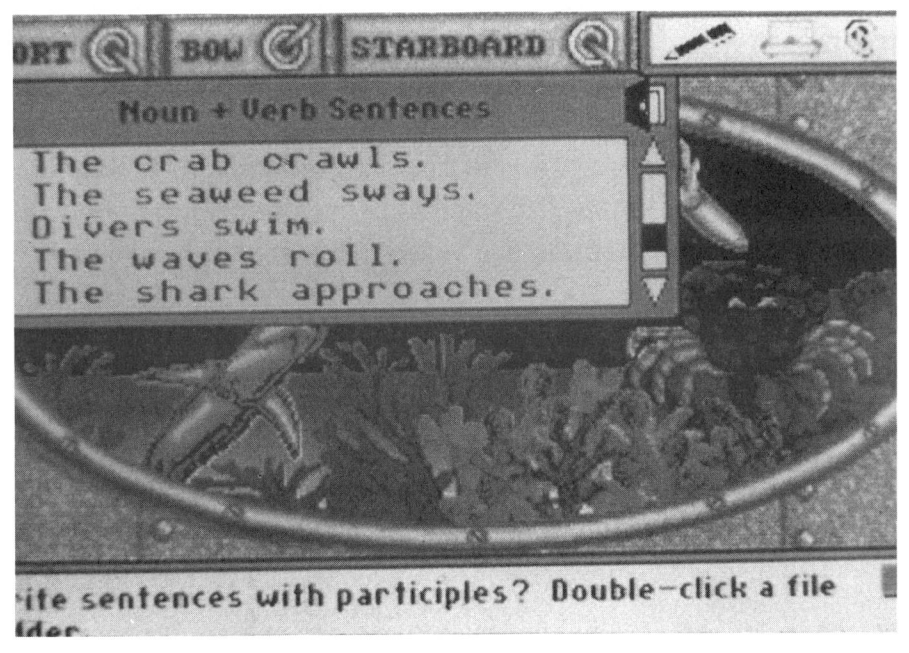

Teens do schoolwork on home computers using CD-ROM educational software. (Photo courtesy I.B.M.)

reality environments to the computer. Three-dimensional software technology creates true stereo 3-D still images and movies.

Gross tells why many of Knowledge Adventure's software products focus on playing games with information and chart data: "There's nothing more powerful than having that light bulb go on in your head when you realize something on your own. Not only do you never forget something you've learned that way, but you carry that excitement about education to other topics.

"In Dinosaur Adventure, for example, we provided the latitudes and longitudes of where dinosaurs used to live. We didn't say that many were in mountain ranges. When players of the game discovered that for themselves, some were so excited they wrote in to tell us about it."

Since learning that one-third of those who buy Knowledge Adventure games are adults, Gross is developing a line of adult educational products on topics such as hobbies, music, art, and adult education.

For those of any age who enjoy cartoons, Main Street Books, a division of Doubleday, offers two interactive CD-ROM disks that present their educational information in cartoon format. The Cartoon History of the Universe traces history from the birth of the planet to Alexander the Great. Volume II covers the beginnings of China to the fall of the Roman Empire.

Jonathan Spence, who teaches modern Chinese history at Yale University in New Haven, Connecticut, believes there is a definite place for cartoon treatments of history and rates the two edutainment disks as legitimate learning tools.

The next step in on-line communication is incorporating full-motion video on an on-line service. (Photo courtesy I.B.M.)

Says Spence: "If large segments of the population are drifting toward virtual illiteracy as they acquire new types of skills through handling computer technology, and if we want to keep alive the idea that history has meaning, then cartoon books and CD-ROM sets like (this) might end up becoming lifelines, rather than mere diversions. And thus, 'splat,' 'pow,' 'ouch,' and 'whoof,' along with whatever has by then replaced the mouse, will end up as our descendants' last points of entry back into the inner mysteries of their pasts." The same might be said of potential "virtual reality" illiteracy.

Are edutainment products just fun and games, or are they legitimate educational supplements? The answer is, some are and some aren't. Some software makers emphasize the fun and games, while others incorporate more challenging features into their programs.

Many parents and educators hope that while young people play computer and video games, they also learn something. Edutainment producers who will succeed in the edutainment market will be those who best combine education with entertainment. Carmen Sandiego led the way for edutainment along the information superhighway. It will be interesting to see where "she" and others go from here.

8

Look, Ma, I'm On-line!

When the U.S. space shuttle *Discovery* hovered near a Russian space station 240 miles above Brazil early in 1995, a computer scientist in Palo Alto, California, not only watched the dramatic event on his office desktop computer, but heard the voices of the astronauts. The miracle of stellar audio and video communications was possible because the computer was attached to the global web of computer networks known as the Internet.

"The means by which the scientist watched and heard the historic space rendezvous was an emerging technology called the M-bone, which is turning the Internet into a virtual broadcasting medium," reports technology writer Peter H. Lewis in the *New York Times*. The M-bone is the Internet's multicast backbone, which functions as a network based on the Internet's framework.

> "The means by which the scientist watched and heard the historic space rendezvous was an emerging technology called the M-bone, which is turning the Internet into a virtual broadcasting medium."

M-bone is virtually a global video telephone system that allows groups of people to share voice, data, and images in "real time" over the Internet. It is an exciting example of how far audio and video technology has come.

People used to write letters to communicate with each other over distances, until the telephone was invented. After World War II, ham (individually operated) radios replaced telephones for thousands of people.

In the 1970s, many ham radio operators began switching to citizens band (CB) radios whose signal length lies between shortwave broadcast and 10-meter amateur radio bands. Over their CB radios, truck drivers alerted each other to where bargain-priced gas stations could be found, and where highway police might be patrolling. Soon, tens of thousands of non-truck drivers began discovering the many pleasures and uses of CB radios, including keeping in touch with others over distances.

The development of the transistor and other micro-electric devices led to the invention of cellular radios that expand distances over which people can communicate by car or home radio. Just as this technology began to take hold, an even newer form of electronic communication arrived, called "on-line." Through the combined use of a computer, a modem attachment, and telephone, users can communicate by voice over vast distances and at the same time transmit or receive printed information on their computer screens.

Millions of people all over the world are subscribing to on-line services such as CompuServe, Prodigy, and America Online that provide "networking" with other users to exchange voice and printed communication. Subscribers receive a variety of services includinig electronic mail, conferencing

> Through the combined use of a computer, a modem attachment, and telephone, users can communicate by voice over vast distances and at the same time transmit or receive printed information on their computer screens.

62 ENTERTAINMENT

support, and interactive magazines and newspapers. They also can access to the Internet, an international network of computers, many of them located in public libraries, universities, and government research facilities. Internet users agree to use the same connecting software so they can communicate with each other electronically.

Who are the estimated 20 million people around the world who are already on-line? They are practically every type of person, from teenagers to the homeless, as Barbara Kantrowitz reports in *Newsweek*. They go on-line to do scientific research, hold political debates, and get stock market tips, advice for the lovelorn, and astrology predictions. People who have been adopted look for, and sometimes find, their birth parents. Sports fans analyze their favorite team's record.

On-line users are everywhere. Rik Tilton, 20, though homeless in California, carries his portable computer with him to log on regularly. He says he keeps sane by sending poems over the network and taking part in on-line conferences on "being alone." In Atqasuk, Alaska, an Eskimo village of 260 people reachable only by airplane, a school building manager, Bryan Lockwood, keeps in touch with the outside world through various computer bulletin boards and takes part in political debates on the Internet.

"Being on-line is like having pen pals, except there's an almost immediate response," says Don Beaver, a single parent who networks with others like him.

One recent addition to the entertainment services of the Internet is the Walt Disney Company's Movie Plex. This interactive service allows users to see previews and clips of Disney movies, read about the making of the company's new films, check the release dates of individual films, learn about special events and premieres, and play movie trivia games.

Perhaps the most exciting new development in on-line communication is the effort to bring full-motion video to an on-line service. Steve Case, who founded America Online in 1985, predicts that within a few years, video will be offered for downloading by subscribers and/or trading live-action video clips with each other in a form of video E-Mail. There also will be video and software that his company or other servers will provide for people to use. Camcorder users will be able to send E-Mail by hooking the unit up to their personal computer, to capture and transmit video over computers.

The "virtual community" that being on-line has created is expanding greatly with the new World Wide Web. Early in 1995, the Prodigy on-line information service became the first consumer computer network to open its electronic system to the popular Internet service known as the World Wide Web. The Web allows even computer novices to easily search the global Internet network for text, pictures, and sound.

"The Web is emerging rapidly as the point-and-click (computer-accessed) prototype for the information superhighway," says Peter H. Lewis, the *New York Times* technology writer. This became evident after Microsoft Corporation, the leading computer software company, announced it would include an optional connection to the Web in its future products, including its Windows operating system that is used in tens of millions of personal computers.

Meanwhile, Prodigy's leading rivals, including CompuServe and America Online, disclosed plans to offer Web access to their millions of subscribers. This, says Lewis, could turn the global computer network into a truly mass medium. Consumers spent $13 billion on the network in 1994.

The key to the Web is hyper-linking, a technology that permits a publisher to create links among related documents, regardless of where on the computer network they physically reside. For example, someone reading a Web article on travel might click on a highlighted phrase referring to the South Pole, and be automatically connected to a computer in New Zealand that offers products and services to Arctic travelers. The Web is being touted as an electronic blending of the public library, the suburban shopping mall, and the *Congressional Record*.

> The Web is being touted as an electronic blending of the public library, the suburban shopping mall, and the *Congressional Record*.

The Web is a system of viewing information, much of it containing graphics and video, stored on tens of thousands of network servers connected to the Internet. At the Web's core is a system known as hypertext linking that makes it easy for people to move from one related document to another without having to know or care where in the world the information is stored.

Among the growing numbers of those going on-line are teenagers who find it to be even more fun than talking with a friend on the telephone for an hour. For some, it can be a lifeline to the outside world. This was the case for a girl whose parents grounded her for skipping homework for a week; the ultimate punishment was removing the modem from her home computer so she couldn't go on-line.

Lucky students at Centennial Middle School in Boulder, Colorado, have their own account on the Internet. At school and at home, many teens spend two to four hours a day on-line, checking their electronic mail, playing interactive games and chatting into the night, writes Scott McCartney in *The Wall Street Journal*.

Centennial students say they prefer going on-line to using the school's traditional teen bulletin board. They communicate better over the networking services that have special "kids only" areas catering to teens.

"It's a lot easier to communicate on-line," says one teenage girl at the school. "We talk about life. We talk about anything and everything."

A boy classmate says, "It's easier to talk to girls on the Internet than in school. Sometimes I can't talk well in person. It doesn't come out like I want. But it does when I'm on-line."

"I've seen students blossom in this environment (on-line) who would normally be withdrawn," says Nancy Songer, assistant professor of education at the University of Colorado at Boulder.

At Skyline High School in Dallas, Texas, the on-line service is an internal school bulletin board that is based in a computer behind one teacher's desk. One of its most popular features is the dating section, where teens can approach schoolmates about going out. One student even went on-line to get advice from classmates about how to break up with her boyfriend.

Is it becoming a peer pressure thing to be on-line? "Kids who have modems are cooler," admits one boy who is pressuring his parents for Internet access from home.

John Prismon, a senior at Boulder High School, says he has lived on-line for four years. A big fan of the "Star Trek" television series, he says living on-line has some of the same "futuristic world" qualities that are so appealing to him on the starship *Enterprise*. "But the only thing that matters," he maintains, "is how a person thinks."

Some may consider computer-modem networking to be little more than a more modernized electronic version of talking over a ham or CB radio. However, the broader uses for information sending and gathering of on-line services appear to make the technology much more important to many more people. Communicating with others and accessing information by going on-line appears to be one of the fastest growing and most significant aspects of the information superhighway.

9

Movie Magic: Digital Special Effects

Seeing may be believing, but today our eyes can play a great many tricks on us at the movies. Since the first motion pictures, moviemakers have found technological ways to make the imagined a reality, at least on film. But today's computer-driven digital special effects are putting things on screen that are almost beyond belief, such as the lifelike dinosaurs in *Jurassic Park* and, in *The Crow*, digitally placing the late Brandon Lee in scenes filmed after his death.

To create the special effects for *Jurassic Park*, Steven Spielberg hired four of the leading F/X technicians in the business: Stan Winston, Dennis Muren, Michael Lantieri, and Phil Tippett. Winston created large-scale mechanical creations for *Aliens* and *Terminator 2: Judgment Day*. Muren is effects supervisor for George Lucas' Industrial Light and Magic (ILM), the company that invented computer-generated special effects. Lantieri, a specialist in physical effects, worked on *Who Framed Roger Rabbit*, the movie that amazingly blended live action with cartoon animation. Tippett

Movie special effects can be realized with the Video Toaster and LightWave 3D to create the most sophisticated movie graphics. (Photo courtesy NewTek)

originated the "go-motion" process, a computerized upgrade of stop-motion animation.

An initial step was to design a new kind of mobile dinosaur, more birdlike than many of the huge lumbering species. Winston's animators were aided by Jack Horner, professor of paleontology at Montana State University. He used powerful computer imaging software to study dinosaur fossils to show how they looked and lived. The images were transformed into three-dimensional forms from which artists worked to create the lifelike prehistoric creatures seen in the movie.

Artists and model makers then created life-sized dinosaurs that were mechanically manipulated by rods, wires, and hydraulic systems. Computer graphics technicians created images that looked incredibly real, then worked with stop-motion animators to make the creatures move in lifelike ways.

The computer graphics team worked on 52 separate shots in the film, including the remarkably realistic "stampede" sequence. Together, they won Academy Awards for best achievement in special effects. Some of the technology-created dinosaurs are on display in the *Jurassic Park* exhibit at Universal Studios in Hollywood.

Other digital magic was employed to virtually bring the dead back to life, when further scenes were needed for *The Crow*, after its star, Brandon Lee, had been killed in an accident during filming of the movie. The work was achieved by Dream Quest Images, a special effects company based in Simi Valley, California.

Silicon Graphics workstations and Macintosh computers were used in more than seven scenes for a total of 52 shots that virtually brought Lee back to life, on film. Powerful computers took images

The *Robocop* movie series special effects were created with the Video Toaster and LightWave software technology.
(Photo courtesy NewTek)

MOVIE MAGIC: DIGITAL SPECIAL EFFECTS 69

> "That's the beauty of digital ... It is another advancement in technology that allows us to make the impossible happen."

of the actor from scenes he had been in before his death and put them in others filmed afterward. The work cost an extra $8 million, but the film, which had been budgeted at $15 million, was saved.

The job of resurrecting Lee on film was given to Dream Quest because of the special effects it had produced for the science fiction cult classic, *Blade Runner*, and the adventure film, *Robin Hood: Prince of Thieves*. The work was done through a process called digital compositing.

"That's the beauty of digital," says executive producer Mark Galvin, of Dream Quest. "It is another advancement in technology that allows us to make the impossible happen."

Digital compositing involves removing an image from a frame of film with new photo imaging software called Matador. The image is then enhanced and dropped into a completely different piece of film. Computer-aided shots included taking Lee's face and placing it on the body of another actor, and one in which his face was digitally placed as a reflection in a mirror.

The results were so successful that moviegoers could not tell which scenes were filmed before Lee's death and which were filmed afterward. The movie became a box-office success and was highly praised for its special effects.

Digital wizardry with computer-generated images also created the special effects that allowed actor Jim Carrey to play incredible visual tricks on viewers in *The Mask*. The work also was done at ILM. One of the greatest challenges facing special effects technicians was how to show what happens when Carrey's character swallows a bundle of dynamite. First, the actor held a prop dynamite bundle over his open mouth. Next, he was filmed as if he had just swallowed it with a big gulp.

The film and prop dynamite were taken to ILM where the film was scanned into powerful Silicon Graphics computers. The computers created an image that appeared to be made of wire. A model maker recreated the prop dynamite in the computer and made an elongated computer model of Carrey's jaw. Animators then replaced an image of his jaw with the computer-generated jaw and inserted the dynamite. The final sequence showed Carrey burping flame and smoke, effects that were filmed at ILM. The whole sequence took more than two months to film, cost $75,000, and lasted only 17 seconds on the screen, but it was one of the reasons the movie found a wide audience.

Another way in which computers are making movie magic is in the restoration of a film's original color after years of fading. Dramatic examples of color restoration include *My Fair Lady* and Walt Disney's *Snow White and the Seven Dwarfs*, both of which had degraded badly over a period of years.

Not only had the color faded in *My Fair Lady*, but there were holes and cracks in the film that had to be filled in digitally. Some of the same kinds of high-tech methods were employed that are used by technicians who create special-effects magic in the movies. The restoration was accomplished by Robert A. Harris and James C. Katz, who had earlier restored *Lawrence of Arabia* to its original color and print clarity.

Since the release of *Snow White* in 1937, the film had acquired dust, dirt, scratches, color fading, and other distortions. Before re-releasing it to theaters, the Walt Disney Company recruited the Eastman Kodak Company's Cinisite subsidiary in Burbank, California, to restore the film to its original condition. Cinisite used the latest computer-generated digital imaging technology to electronically scan each of the 119,500 frames of the 83-minute movie, the first full-length animated feature ever made. Capturing it as a computer file required 40 megabytes of data, more than the entire storage system of most home computers. In all, the film required 4.5 billion bytes of information to record.

Each frame was displayed on a computer screen and grime and scratches were electronically removed by Kodak's Vineon software and hardware from Silicon Graphics. After a frame was electronically cleaned and adjusted, it was rerecorded on film using red, blue, and green lasers. With the digital data, accurate copies were made of the film.

"It has always been a filmmaker's dream that a film should be forever," says Ed Jones, the president of Cinesite who supervised the *Snow White* restoration. "We are using computer technology to make that happen."

Computer technology also has enabled movie technicians to restore many films that had deteriorated because they were originally made on nitrate film, which decomposes over time. It also has played a major role in the practice of colorizing movies that originally were made in black and white. The practice began in the mid-1980s to create new markets for many old films.

No one can predict how creative special-effects technicians will amaze us in future movies. Their progress so far, however, makes it a sure thing that we have seen only the beginning of their high-tech wizardry.

10

Home Theaters

Popcorn and soda in hand, you sink into a plush, velvet seat with anticipation as the overture sets the mood. Magically, the lights dim, the music fades, and the curtain opens.

The movie begins and you're enveloped by stunning images and sound of unparalleled clarity. The real world disappears and you're immersed in another place and time.

You're at a movie theater, right? Wrong. You haven't left the comfort and safety of your home. You're in your very own home theater. Welcome to the wonderful new world of home cinema.

Not many years ago, only millionaires and movie stars had theaters in their homes. The rich and famous would gather for private showings of new movies in specially-built minitheaters in mansions. Several thousand other, less affluent movie buffs owned costly and bulky 35mm sound projection equipment on which to show movies in their homes. The movies they played and collected cost several hundred dollars each to buy.

Television changed all that, by transmitting movies to homes without the purchase of specialized motion picture and sound equipment. One could say that every television set provided consumers with their own home theater. Video recorders further advanced the "home theater," allowing consumers to play and collect their own personal libraries of movies to show whenever they wished.

Front-view TV projection such as this ceiling-mounted system can provide theater-sized home movie theater viewing. (Photo courtesy ISR, Inc.)

But owning a television set and video recorder still wasn't the same as having a home theater. Today that is all changing. Advances in video and audio technology are enabling thousands of people to install theaters in their homes.

What equipment is needed, and how much does it cost to have a home theater? First and foremost, a large-screen front-view or rear-view projection set is needed, as well as a high-scale video recorder and/or laser disk player. To create the best sound, a high-tech stereo surround sound system that can involve as many as five or more speakers should be installed. Surprisingly, the total cost may be under $5,000, if you shop wisely and buy from discount appliance stores or warehouse outlets. This equipment simulates as closely as possible having a theater in one's own home.

For those who want a home theater more like the real thing, like a theater with padded seats and chandeliers in the lobby, one must be custom-built. Movie fan Rich Warren, a movie and technology writer for *Video* magazine, recently had his basement remodeled into a state-of-the-art home theater.

Warren contacted THX, an advanced stereo sound subsidiary of Lucasfilm that offers home theater training sessions for dealers and installers, at its Skywalker Ranch in Marin County, California. They invited a consultant and contractor Warren had hired for his project to attend the THX training seminar. Together, they made plans for converting his basement into a high-tech home theater about 23 feet deep by 12 feet wide, with a nearly 7-foot ceiling.

A large equipment room was created against one basement wall and a second wall was built in front of it to hide the television equipment and wiring. Two openings were made in the front wall, for shelves to hold a video recorder, laser disk player, sound equipment,

Top-of-the-line home movie theaters can include several rows of plush seats and even a popcorn machine. (Photo courtesy ISR, Inc.)

videotapes, and laser disks. Speakers were appropriately placed around the room and track lighting with dimming switches was installed.

"While not essential, choosing equipment prior to construction results in a more integrated home theater, electrically, acoustically, and visually," says Warren. "For example, knowing the size and shape of the surround sound speakers determines placement, and thus where the wiring will go, and whether the speakers hang independently or need a shelf."

After comparing many television sets and systems, Warren chose a Toshiba 56-inch TheaterWide widescreen rear projection television set and the B&W THX Home Cinema speaker system. For the rest of his system, he selected the McIntosh C39 Audio/Video Control Center that includes Dolby Pro-Logic and THX processing, a Panasonic LX-900 laser disk player, JVC Super VHS and Sony Super Betamax video recorders, and one of the new RCA DSS satellite dishes to receive the best television picture and sound. Audio, video, lighting, and utility electrical outlets each were wired on independent 20-amp circuits.

Two rows of seats were installed, one slightly higher than the other for optimum viewing. The walls and ceiling were equipped with soundproofing and the floor was carpeted. Finally, the theater was equipped with smoke and water sensors and a fire alarm system.

"The theater took 10 weeks and $22,000 to build," says Warren. "It is filled with components costing about as much, and delivers total satisfaction. A considerable amount could have been saved by selecting less expensive equipment, but corners could not have been cut in the construction.

"You can place $7 in a piggy bank everytime you think of going out to a movie, or include the cost in your mortgage or home improvement loan. Then sit back and discover all the new friends you have."

Contractors who can install custom home theater systems are available in most cities. Some, like Integrated Systems by Rich, in Naperville, Illinois, also build complete home automation systems and business audio-video conference systems.

"Our home theater systems usually cost between 5 and 8 percent of the total cost of the home," says Keith Rich, president of the company.

On the low end, builders are designating space for mini home theaters or entertainment centers in family rooms or master bedrooms, says Jim Sulski, building writer for the *Chicago Tribune*.

"Home theaters are becoming popular as buyers become more savvy about changing electronics and all the bells and whistles of audio and video," says Sulski. "This includes technology like big-screen televisions, projection-screen TVs, surround sound systems with multiple speakers, laser disk and videotape players and an array of audio equipment."

> "Home theaters are becoming popular as buyers become more savvy about changing electronics and all the bells and whistles of audio and video."

The cost of a very adequate home theater system can range from $4,000 to $8,000, depending on which audio-video components a buyer chooses. A built-in home entertainment center with 50-inch television set can cost about $3,200, and the buyer supplies any other components.

For those with the total effect in mind, a home theater can come complete with popcorn, soda, and candy machines.

Both installers of home theater systems and home builders are confident that home theater and home entertainment systems that incorporate the latest multimedia and interactive features of computers will be more common features in homes of the future. Also, home theaters are just one aspect of how advanced technology will be included in new homes of today and tomorrow. Besides operating home entertainment systems, electronic home management systems can operate and monitor indoor and outdoor lighting, heating and cooling, security and video surveillance cameras, garage and entrance doors and gates, sprinkler systems, and telephones and other in-home communications.

"All of these time-savers and safeguards are operated through a central computer 'brain,'" says Keith Rich. "They [electronic home management systems] are provided by advanced, customized computer software combined with automation technology. They provide a system that truly reflects and responds to a person's lifestyle needs. With the touch of a button or a simple phone call, you set in motion a series of activities that otherwise would require more of your time and physical effort."

If you really want a home theater like one of the movie palaces of years ago, Rich will install a marquee in your home theater with a cinema name of your choice, such as "Pete's Movie Palace." Authentic movie poster displays can be added, as well as a concession stand with commercial popcorn popper and candy. Even a box office at the entrance to your home theater can be set up, where guests might be charged a small fee to help pay for the theater.

> "They [electronic home management systems] are provided by advanced, customized computer software combined with automation technology. They provide a system that truly reflects and responds to a person's lifestyle needs."

"Why go out to the movies?," asks Rich. "Home cinema is luxurious, intimate, and without the hassles of parking, unwanted noise, and close contact with complete strangers. It's the ultimate in visual and sound quality. It's the ultimate environment for enjoying today's entertainment." And the chance of finding gum on the seat is far less than at commercial movie houses.

For those who want to keep up with the latest in home theater technology, there is a magazine devoted just to that: *Home Theater*, published by Triple D Publishing in Shelby, North Carolina.

For many movie and television enthusiasts, having their own home theater is the ultimate in electronic entertainment.

78 ENTERTAINMENT

11

Rock Goes Interactive

Nothing sent 300,000 rock fans higher into orbit at Woodstock '94 than the digital world of multimedia that was seen by those who ventured behind the main concert area at Saugerties, New York. In a 6-acre area dubbed Surreal Field, major music and computer technology companies such as Philips and Apple demonstrated hands-on exhibits of the latest interactive music technology.

"Philips ruled Surreal Field with one of the most elaborate multimedia displays we've ever seen," reported Brent Butterworth in *Video* magazine. "Each morning, festival-goers lined up beneath a giant dinosaur with outmoded electronics—eight-track tape players and the like—hanging from its four-story skeleton. A looped voice whispered, 'Behold. Don't get frozen in the past. Step into the future.'"

The dinosaur led to a theater where an introduction to Philips' CD-i played on dozens of monitors and two huge projection television screens. After viewing a film, media enthusiasts could settle in among 90 CD-i play stations in a nearby tent and listen to and play along with the latest in interactive music.

For many, the highlight of the exhibit was a performance by rock musician Todd Rundgren, who specializes in using interactive

> Thanks to the latest computer and music simulation technology, would-be rock stars can play guitar, piano, or sing along with some of the top recording and performance artists. Fans can even go into cyberspace with them on the Internet.

technology in his shows. He performed in a "Todd Pod," a compact interactive stage set that looked like an open-air Apollo space capsule. Audiences were able to participate in the spontaneous creation of music. Video cameras were lowered into the crowd during the performance and fed real-time images to monitors mounted across the top of the Pod.

The technology unveiled at Woodstock '94 taps into today's twin emphasis in music—multimedia and interactive. What could be more fun than listening to a favorite rock band? Why, sure, being part of it. Thanks to the latest computer and music simulation technology, would-be rock stars can play guitar, piano, or sing along with some of the top recording and performance artists. Fans can even go into cyberspace with them on the Internet.

The Rolling Stones with Mick Jagger and Keith Richards became the first major rock band to go on-line live on the Internet when they aired a 20-minute audio and video broadcast from the Cotton Bowl in Dallas, Texas to millions of fans seated at their home computers. It was a publicity stunt to promote their longer pay-per-view concert on the cable station Showtime.

A drawback to selling rock over the Internet is the high cost to consumers. Since high-quality sound reproduction takes a high-end computer, known as a work station, which can cost up to $20,000, as well as a modem and telephone connection, few computers other than those at universities and corporations have access to it. While only about 200 computer sites logged on for the Rolling Stones preview concert, some were from as far away as Iceland and New Zealand.

How well did the picture and sound show up on computer screens? *New York Times* reporter Neil Strauss wrote that the picture filled only a fraction of the screen, about 1½ inches square, and picture quality was poor. Reportedly, the sound was "very choppy."

Typical of what can happen in computer networking, the Stones were one-upped by a little-known band, Severe Tire Damage. The group learned that the channel carrying the Stones was open to anyone, so it broadcast an impromptu performance from the Xerox PARC offices in Palo Alto, California, directly before and after the Stones' concert.

> "The Internet has become the biggest promotional tool for the music industry since the invention of the press release."

"The Internet has become the biggest promotional tool for the music industry since the invention of the press release," says Neil Strauss. Nearly every major and independent record company has gone on-line to promote its bands and stars. Some offer fans live chat sessions with their favorites over the Internet.

Aerosmith claimed to be the first rock group to offer one of its single records exclusively on-line, although a service called the Internet Underground Music Archive had already made some 75 songs available only on the Internet. Many consider "Internet record stores" for computer home-shoppers to be the next step in the music industry's evolution.

Some computer and music enthusiasts predict that in five years people will either buy custom-cut CDs with songs taken from the Internet or not go to the record store at all and copy songs onto disks at home right off the Internet. Whether rock music has a future on the Internet will depend on improved technology to produce better pictures and sound.

Meanwhile, more music fans are interacting with their favorite rock stars by means of other entertainment technologies. About 10 million Americans had computers with CD-ROM drives or Philips CD-i (Compact Disk interactive) players in 1995, and that number is expected to rise to 15 to 20 million by 1996. Hooked up to high-tech audio equipment, and paying $25 to $100 for individual music disks, anyone can jam with their favorite artist. That's all it takes to get in on Interactive Rock.

Besides Woodstock '94, Todd Lundgren enjoyed a big success with "No World Order," the first "do-it-yourself" rock album. Listeners with CD-i players could customize any of the 10 tracks to their tastes, changing tempo and mood, or creating new sounds.

Another favorite rocker, David Bowie, jumped on the interactive bandwagon with appropriately-named "Jump: David Bowie Interactive," that allowed fans to create their own music videos using songs from his *Black Tie White Noise* album. "It's like you're playing a live TV producer with five cameras," says software designer Ty Roberts.

For Elvis Presley fans, the King lives on through CD-ROM. On Crunch Media's disk, Virtual Graceland, fans roam freely through Presley's mansion, room by room, and play his hits on his personal phonograph in the TV room. The interactive features even allow users to play his piano and strum his guitar.

Rock music has never been far away from electronic technology, Richard Corliss writes in *Time* magazine: "Technological razzle-jazzle has energized rock music ever since the Moog-and-groove, sound-and-light-show days of the '60s. The synthesizer, a computerized one-man band, has become the instrumental instrument in many a rock group."

Heavy-metal groups like Guns N' Roses and Metallica, as well as megatheatrical performers such as Janet Jackson and David Bowie, have shown that computerized control of stage lighting creates a wide range of special effects. The Grateful Dead keeps things fresh with computerized psychedelia synchronized to the music and projected on big screens. "The aim," says Corliss, "is to find a visual corollary to the spontaneity of live (or Dead) rock 'n' roll."

If playing music and not just listening to others play is your thing, other technology beckons. With Jaminator, for instance, your rock 'n' roll fantasies can become a reality. Jaminator is interactive music with a tangible "air guitar." With digital sounds to simulate rock reality, from the moment users strap on the virtual guitar they can look and sound like they've practiced for years. With a selection of prerecorded band back-ups, just about anyone can play lead guitar with the world's greatest guitar artists. They can jam to any kind of music, from pop to jazz, rock 'n' roll to country.

Jaminator uses digitally recorded instrument sounds for its guitar, keyboard, percussion, and band backgrounds, making the sound quality superior to products using synthesized sounds. Thirty-nine cord controlled riffs produce high quality sounding guitar music, while the built-in keyboard and percussion riffs provide exciting musical accents.

Also available for would-be guitarists is the interactive Virtual Guitar, a guitar with accompanying CD-ROM game that feeds into a multimedia personal computer. The object of the game is to play the Virtual Guitar well enough to progress from soloing in a bedroom to jamming with a real rock band, Aerosmith. It's pretty easy: Players just hit the strings and the computer picks the right chords. A major drawback is that users do not learn alternate picking, but just strumming, so they do not become very accomplished guitarists (that takes more learning and practice in the old-fashioned way that technology cannot provide).

For would-be singers, karaoke has been the answer for several years. The technology allows users to sing along to background music, often with the words and some appropriate visuals shown on a television screen. A cable television channel devoted exclusively to karaoke is in the planning stages. The new channel is to be tested at Time Warner's interactive cable television pilot project in Orlando, Florida.

For those who want to play the piano without really learning, there are many varieties of electronic pianos with built-in rhythms, tempos, and a hundred or more simulated musical instrument sounds. Now comes the "reproducing piano," invented by Wayne Stahnke of Culver City, California. Akin to the player piano of the 1920s, it is a new digital recording piano that uses computer technology to reproduce on compact disk the exact sound of a particular pianist's performance. Many leading piano manufacturers are incorporating the "reproducing pianos'" Piano Disk mechanism into their new models, such as Yamaha's Disklavier concert grand piano. They're guaranteed, too: When you sit down to play like George Shearing, Peter Nero, or even Ignace Jan Paderewski, no one laughs!

Meanwhile, interactive music marches on at the Sony Corporation, Philips Electronics, and Microsoft Corporation. All are working on a manufacturing process that may spur a new generation of music compact disks with interactive features.

Several recording companies are expressing interest in the process. If it catches on, it will make playing multimedia compact disks simpler. A user will be able to play a CD in an audio player and then put the same disk in a computer CD-ROM drive and have access to video interviews, concert films, and other music-related information. The price may be only slightly higher than the cost of today's audio CD.

With a karaoke player, anyone can be a rock singer or musician, interacting with thousands of backup tunes by following lyrics and a video on a TV. (Photo courtesy Pioneer)

Let there be music, and make it as exciting as possible for performers and listeners! That seems to be the challenge facing musicians, recording companies, and manufacturers as computer features such as interactive and multimedia are incorporated more and more into the ever changing world of music.

12

Radio's Role in the Information Revolution

The radio industry is working hard to become a significant player in the information revolution. Ever since the advent of television in the late 1940s and video recorders in the 1970s, radio has acutely felt the competition of advanced visual technology. In recent years, battery-operated portable radios, as well as all-music and all-talk radio, have increased audiences greatly. Radio still enjoys a wide appeal, partly because it is still an information and entertainment medium that millions turn to in their cars and homes, not to mention while they exercise or are at the beach. For many, a Walkman has almost become part of their ears.

One of the newest advances in radio is digital satellite radio, a new technology that eventually will compete with local stations. Early in 1995, the Federal Communications Commission allocated a portion of the airways for satellite radio broadcasting. This created a new class of services, using satellites to beam programs directly to listeners' radios nationwide, and competed with local AM and FM stations. The satellites beam dozens of channels of radio programming in a digital form that matches the clarity of compact disks, well exceeding that of FM and AM stations.

The widespread arrival of digital audio radio (D.A.R.) is still several years away, however. "This is in part because some Commission officials worry about undermining conventional broadcasters and must still define the rules under which the satellite services are allowed to operate," says Edmund L. Andrews, media writer for the *New York Times*. Also, the National Association of Broadcasters, a trade group, and many local stations fear that competition from satellite radio could capture both listeners and a share of the group's advertising revenue.

Meanwhile, the music publishing divisions of the Sony Corporation and Time Warner, as well as Time Warner Cable, have invested about $20 million in Digital Cable Radio of Hatboro, Pennsylvania,

As many as 50 CD-quality music channels are sent to cable and satellite TV customers by way of satellite transmission. (Photo courtesy Music Choice.)

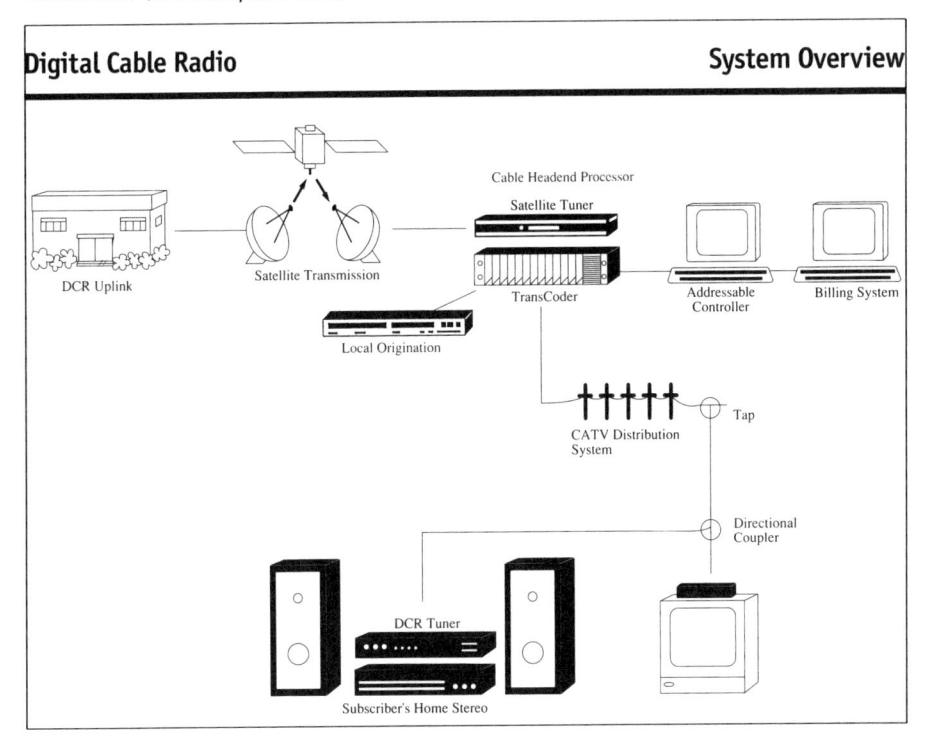

Digital Cable Radio — System Overview

RADIO'S ROLE IN THE INFORMATION REVOLUTION 87

> "Just as cable TV stimulated movie sales, we believe Digital Cable Radio will have a similar effect on recorded music," says Michael P. Schulhof, president of Sony Software Corporation. "It could boost visits to music retail outlets and increase CD sales."

a new pay-radio service transmitted through local cable television systems. Listeners would pay a subscription fee of about $10 a month to access more than 50 channels. Within a few years, channels could increase to about 250, including news, sports, talk shows, and foreign-language programming. Digital Cable Radio is already available in Mexico, and there are plans to introduce it in Europe, East Asia, and Latin America.

The objections to cable radio in this country are similar to those against satellite radio. Some in the music publishing business fear that cable radio services offering talk-free, compact-disk-quality music could hurt CD sales because more people may engage in home taping rather than buying pre-recorded disks. Advocates of digital radio disagree, saying cable radio could help record companies by serving, in effect, as advertising, and helping to create an awareness of new artists.

"Just as cable TV stimulated movie sales, we believe Digital Cable Radio will have a similar effect on recorded music," says Michael P. Schulhof, president of Sony Software Corporation. "It could boost visits to music retail outlets and increase CD sales."

Meanwhile, thanks to talk radio coming to computers, radio is alive and well on the Internet, the global computer network that links more than 10 million people, from teenagers to scientists, academics, engineers, and high-tech industry executives.

"Listening to a talk show via computer instead of a radio might seem merely a digital curiosity," says John Markoff, media writer for the *New York Times*, "but many computer scientists and telecommunications experts believe it signals the first step in a transformation in which national and even global computer networks will fiercely compete with, or even replace, traditional television and radio networks that broadcast over the air or transmit by cable."

"Internet Talk Radio," broadcast from Arlington, Virginia, beginning in March, 1993, became the first such service. Internet users obtain it as a file of computer data, just as they might "download" from the network a research report, data about a scientific experiment, or any of thousands of other data files. Listeners hear the program as it is transmitted or store the data in their computers and play it back later.

"We're not all going to start listening to radio on our computers yet," says Paul Saffo, a computer industry analyst at the Institute for the Future, in Menlo Park, California. "But it has many possibilities." Some predict that digital cable radio can increasingly compete with conventional media like television, radio, and newspapers.

A video version of digital cable radio also might be carried on the Internet. "It's a brilliant idea," says Nicholas Negroponte, director of the Media Laboratory, a computer research center at Massachusetts Institute of Technology in Cambridge. "Newspapers, radio, and television are really in the same business. We've always thought video or audio or data are different businesses. But today, when you radiate bits, those bits don't have to have a specific medium attached to them."

Blending the power of the computer with conventional radio or television could create an intriguing new medium that will give viewers or listeners more control over what they receive, while allowing them to interact with the medium in a manner not now possible. "Conceivably, any Internet user could create his or her own audio or video program that could be made available on the network," says Markoff.

About a year after the debut of "Internet Talk Radio," a 24-hour radio station began broadcasting over the Internet. The Internet Multicasting Company of Washington, D.C., a nonprofit enterprise formed to develop new uses for computer-based communications, began broadcasting by Internet early in 1995. It serves people who would rather watch their computers instead of

> "Conceivably, any Internet user could create his or her own audio or video program that could be made available on the network."

listening to conventional radio or watching television. The broadcasts are transmitted globally, and can be stored, searched, and augmented with text and picture files. In some cases, listeners can retrieve biographical data about the speakers and send them comments by electronic mail.

Radio Internet broadcasts live gavel-to-gavel audio broadcasts from the U.S. Congress, performances at the Kennedy Center for the Performing Arts, speeches from the National Press Club, and recordings of famous authors reading their books. The talk radio station's most popular feature is "Geek of the Week." Since, in the Internet community, "geek" is someone who has highly advanced technical skills, the word is meant to be complimentary.

So far, only a few thousand people worldwide have the high-speed network data capacity, or bandwidth, necessary to listen to live audio transmissions over their computers. But millions of Internet subscribers with standard personal computers and regular telephone lines will be able to retrieve pieces of the radio transmissions. This can be accessed from repositories in Radio Technology for Mankind, a "cyberstation" that carries the broadcasts.

On another technology front, efforts are being made to incorporate interactive features into radios. David J. Alwadish, a New York City businessman, uses a little-used technology called the radio data system (R.D.S.) to transform car radios into interactive conduits. They make it possible for listeners, radio stations, and advertisers to exchange information, requests, and promotions.

R.D.S. technology allows a radio station to transmit data on the unused portion of its frequency, known as a subcarrier. Alwadish created "Coupon Radio," a car radio system in which listeners can "capture" radio information with the push of a button. It gives radio stations and advertisers—such as record companies and music stores—information about listeners' habits and tastes.

The information is recorded on a "smart card," like a plastic credit card, that is inserted into a recording device built into the radio. The data on the card can be displayed on a narrow radio screen or taken into a store where a coupon can be issued electronically or printed out, using a credit card printer.

"Coupon Radio brings radio into the twenty-first century," says Alwadish. "It is about the American automobile, the American retailer, and the American broadcaster being linked interactively."

Ready or not, R.D.S. is showing up more and more on your car radio's station identification screen. Radio industry technologists are hoping to persuade listeners to interact more with their radios by printing messages on the small display screens of car radios. These may be a station's call letters, a song's title and artist, and traffic and weather bulletins. Sports buffs can search for all the sports programming in a city with the push of a button. A "handoff" function automatically tunes the radio to a stronger station playing the same program.

"This new technology will bring an exciting, useful, and cost-effective new service to the radio listener," says Almon Clegg, chairman of a committee sponsored by electronics manufacturers and broadcasters to develop the R.D.S. system in this country.

Radio, far from being a dead medium, is showing new life in these and many other new ways. Digital data displayed on a car radio screen may give us much-needed information while we're driving, but at a risk. Skeptics wonder how long it will be before advertising messages appear on our car's dashboard radio monitor.

13

Interactive Sports Technology
– A Whole New Ballgame

There is a lot more going on for sports fans in the information revolution than just having video store shelves full of instructional tapes on how to play tennis, golf, or lose 10 pounds by stair-stepping and doing aerobics to Chubby Checker songs. Sports viewing is going interactive.

Let's say you and your best friend were two of the biggest sports fans on the East Coast. For years, together you watched all your favorite college and professional basketball and football teams at local stadiums or on television. But when your friend moved to California, all that ended. You sit in front of your television set and he sits in front of his and you watch the same game, but a couple of thousand miles apart. Afterward, you share excitement about a great dunk shot or touchdown, but by telephone.

Soon, thanks to the combined technologies of television, telephone, and telecommunications, that may change. Sports fans will communicate with each other via interactive satellite video. This will be made possible by two high-capacity wires or cables that will run into every home and business office. Customers will choose which conduit to use for phone calls, electronic text on computers, video, music, or some multimedia information marvel combining them all. One of the most intriguing prospects for the technology is that it will enable sports fans to communicate and interact with each other across great distances. All of this will be made possible by the joint ventures or mergers of some of the nation's major telephone and telecommunications companies working together to bring new interactive capabilities to computers and television sets.

While watching a televised football game in his home in New York City, a fan can watch it simultaneously with a friend in Los Angeles. "What do you think of that pass interception?" the East Coast football fan can ask his West Coast friend, talking by long-distance telephone into a speaker in his television set. "His right foot was over the line," his West Coast friend complains. "The ref was blind to call it a fair catch." Both sports fans also can supplement their viewing with digitized records of past football games from a video archive and team statistics from a remote data base.

New technology already is changing the way people watch sports on television. For example, a viewer becomes tired of watching a baseball game from the center-field camera the network chooses. A click of a remote control device switches the view to behind home plate. Then the viewer wonders how much the batter who just struck out earns. Another click and the answer appears on the screen: $2 million a year.

These are just some of the new interactive capabilities sports viewers already enjoy in Canada through a service called Videoway, and similar services may soon become available in America. "And we ain't seen nothing yet," says John Helyar in *The Wall Street Journal*. "Although much of the talk of television's future programming content centers on cinema, the voracious appetite of the 500-channel satellite TV system will make sports of vital importance as well."

"The TV landscape is going to be changing in the next five or ten years, and sports leagues will be a big part of that," says Gary Bettman, National Hockey League commissioner. Several interactive TV services are already in play, using sports as a primary attraction.

Sega's NBA '95 brings professional basketball action to life in video game play. (Photo courtesy Sega)

One of these services, appropriately named Interactive TV, "allows viewers to do by high-tech means what they have long done with low-tech shouts," says Helyar. "They can predict the next play and match wits not only with the coaches but also with thousands of other viewers."

For satellite television fans, a bonanza of games is available, even those blacked out (not broadcast locally). The National Football League began offering a service called "Sunday Ticket" to satellite subscribers for the 1994 football season. Fans who wanted more than just watching the NFL's five televising networks tapped into every game via satellite, at a total cost of $99 to see every game their favorite team played that season.

DirecTV, the satellite service, reserves 30 of its approximately 150 channels for sports, giving viewers a wide range of choices each night. Also, more sports channels devoted to individual sports are being offered, such as horse and auto racing. The Golf Channel, offering 24-hour coverage of live and taped tournaments and golfing tips began telecasting over satellite early in 1995, for a monthly fee of about $7.

While many believe viewers will go wild over interactive sports via television, others are more cautious. "People use sports to relax," says Steven Bornstein, president of the cable and satellite sports network, ESPN. "They don't want to roam around the whole TV universe. They want to see the best game. Most of those will continue to be on the major networks."

As for calling the shots in a football game, Gary Arlen, a Bethesda, Maryland, interactive technology consultant, has his doubts. "After you control the cameras and miss every play for a while," he says, "you come to realize the value of a professional director." Still, it can be fun to play sports TV director at home.

Meanwhile, another new company, Sportslab Inc., based in San

Pro football can be enjoyed year-round with Sega's NFL '95 video game. (Photo courtesy Sega)

> "After you control the cameras and miss every play for a while, you come to realize the value of a professional director."

Francisco, has taken another lead in the interactive TV sports campaign. It recently started an interactive, multimedia traveling sports education show to encourage families to get more involved in recreational activities.

Sportslab assembles a wide variety of electronic sports exhibits and demonstrations dealing with football, basketball, and tennis, as well as hang-gliding and mountain biking. Fans interact with the exhibits in huge tents. These tents and technology are moved from city to city. Sports educational tools include video games or "virtual reality" equipment that simulates a sport or activity.

For on-line sports fans, the Sports/Leisure Magazines Group of the New York Times Company is teaming with the Unet 2 Corporation, an electronic publisher specializing in on-line consumer services, to begin an on-line sports network for computer users. Sports fans signing onto the computer network will be able to access information and photos in *Golf World, Tennis, Snow Country, Cruising World*, and *Sailing World*. Subscribers also will be able to communicate with each other, receive instructions from experts in a variety of sports, and look at classified advertisements to buy sports equipment.

When a favorite sport is out of season, there are hundreds of computer floppy disks and CD-ROMs to put fans into just about any game or sport. One such game is Joe Montana's NFL Football CD from Sega, a three-dimensional behind-the-quarterback view of the game. A vivid soundtrack surrounds the player, including the crunch of pads, and the football legend himself coaches in digitized video commentary.

For golfers, the game still can be played in a blizzard during the dead of winter, with a little help from computer and video technology. In many major cities such as Chicago, golfers can go to places like Windy City Golf. With a few button punches on video equipment, golfers can play a round of indoor golf in front of a large-screen television, monitored by video cameras. A computer tells how long a golfer's drive was, and whether a shot was hooked or sliced.

The video golf lesson costs about $25 an hour or $30 for a foursome to play the virtual reality course that simulates playing on a well-known course. The computer also has a split-screen that allows players to compare their swing to that of a pro.

Technology also is going out to the ballgame. It isn't enough to go to a baseball game, listen to it on a radio headset, or watch it on a small-screen portable TV set. Now fans can watch a game from the bleachers with a hand-held battery-operated computer called Rotisserie that provides instant statistical information derived from vast data bases where millions of bits of baseball news, trivia, and analysis are stored.

What is there for sportswomen in the information revolution? Two companies are vying for the lead in cable telecasting specially aimed at women sports fans: Women's Sports Network and Liberty Sports. Having two stations devoted to women's sports appeals to Donna Lopiano, executive director of the Women's Sports Foundation. "We haven't found that any of the networks have touched the needs of women interested in health, exercise, and sports," says Ms. Lopiano.

Since sports and politics are the nation's two national pastimes, it is almost certain that the information revolution will play a major role in how sports are watched and played. The emphasis is already being placed on bringing sports into the multimedia and interactive age, and, as one technology expert has implied, the best is yet to come.

14

Privacy, Piracy, and Pranks in the Information Age

Vast amounts of personal information are stored in computer data banks, and much of it is easily accessed by just about anyone, for proper or improper use. Also, as more people use computers to store and retrieve information for various home uses, including entertainment, and millions more go on-line to communicate by computers and modems, the concerns about safeguarding personal privacy become greater. An individual's privacy is put at risk as more information becomes public . . . as computer networks replace traditional gathering places such as the workplace, the school, the shopping mall, and the movie theater, and the home becomes both the workplace and playground of more people.

Invention of the telegraph shortened distances of communicating, and the telephone further intruded on the privacy of the home. Now the blending of media, computers, telephones, and cellular, satellite, and microwave transmission technology is virtually putting the world in our hands, in the forms of computer keyboards, TV remote controls, or telephone handsets. Some people abuse this easy access to information about others to invade their privacy.

Is privacy in the information revolution a real issue or an imagined one? Americans of all ages divide sharply on whether computers and other technologies are being used to invade personal privacy. Fifty-five percent of those surveyed in a 1994 study by the Times Mirror Center for the People and the Press expressed concern about privacy. Sophisticated computer users voiced worry about privacy less often (47 percent) than those who never use a computer (57 percent).

"Privacy may not be possible," says Louis Rosetto, editor and publisher of *Wired* magazine, a leader in the information technology field. "We take privacy for granted because we believe it is guaranteed by our laws and because mass society confers upon us a certain anonymity.

"But technology is eroding our privacy. Our financial, medical, [and] political records all are accessible to whoever wants to know. The

Computer and telecommunications users may risk invasion of privacy and misuse of their on-line identification. (Photo courtesy I.B.M.)

> "We take privacy for granted because we believe it is guaranteed by our laws and because mass society confers upon us a certain anonymity. But technology is eroding our privacy... The Global Village has its downside. In a village, everyone knows everyone else's business."

Global Village (communicating on-line) has its downside. In a village, everyone knows everyone else's business."

"Privacy is a tradeoff we make every day in life, whenever we confide in someone on delicate tasks," says Nicholas Negroponte, director of the Massachusetts Institute of Technology's Media Laboratory. "We forfeit privacy against the risk. Computers are different in that we often don't know we are handing over such information, and its subsequent use can be shocking."

Perhaps the most publicized example of this was a fake news release late in 1994. Under the guise of an Associated Press news article, the release to thousands of computers around the world declared that the Microsoft Corporation had agreed to acquire the Roman Catholic Church in exchange for "an unspecified number of shares of Microsoft common stock." The release was a prank, the idea of an anonymous person who could not be traced, but it received worldwide attention before Microsoft exposed the release as a hoax.

In another example, at the Massachusetts Institute of Technology in Cambridge, unknown and untraceable computer pirates illegally traded copyrighted software through a computer bulletin board. Prosecutors described it as one of the most active network sites in the multibillion-dollar market for pirated software.

These and other cases of misuse of the information superhighway cause concern about a new form of electronic money which soon may be used on computer networks. Called "digital cash," the high-tech money could become the basic currency for new forms of on-line shopping and commerce. But law enforcement officials fear it also could lead to virtually untraceable new forms of illegal financial transactions.

Meanwhile, for parents of younger children, user-guard and safety devices are being installed on computers and other information technology. Some of the devices, like the "Child Guardian" transmitter, allow a parent to beep a child. The child then can sound an alarm with his receiver. Similar devices are "Child Sentry" and "Beeper Kid," enabling parents or guardians to electronically monitor the whereabouts and safety of their children.

The latest major examples of eavesdropping and theft in the information revolution have been occurring on the Internet. Federal computer security agents in San Francisco discovered that unknown intruders developed a new way to break into computer systems on the global Internet.

Companies and individuals connected to the Internet reported that intruders, posing as "friendly" computers, break into computers and computer networks and steal data and security codes. The intruders also are able to gain access to normally secure networks by finding and then using the identity of a computer that a network recognizes as being an authorized user.

Unless computer users take complicated measures to protect themselves and their data banks, an intruder could copy or destroy documents or even operate undetected by posing as an authorized user of the system. Since computer intruders could literally steal credit card numbers, merchandise, and money, it's like burglars having master keys to all the doors of the homes in an entire neighborhood.

> Since computer intruders could literally steal credit card numbers, merchandise, and money, it's like burglars having master keys to all the doors of the homes in an entire neighborhood.

"These guys are striking the basis of trust that makes the network work, and I hate that," says Marcus Ranum, a senior scientist at Trusted Information Services, a computer security firm.

As computer and telecommunications technology becomes even more complex and widely used, privacy and safety are certain to grow as concerns in the information revolution. So far, for every clever invader of computer and on-line privacy there has been an even more clever technology expert to detect and repel the invasion.

There are ways to prevent "superhighway robbery" on the Internet. Network security advisers suggest that if someone calls claiming to be from your network service provider investigating a security problem, if they ask for your password, it's usually a scam. Also, you may give your name to strangers you meet on-line, but never your address or phone number, because you may not know if they can be trusted with that information. Also, pick a proper password for networking. Avoid using names, birthdays, or recognizable words. Instead, use a combination of numbers, letters, and symbols that protect your true identity.

The basis for solving the problems of privacy, piracy, and pranks are the time-honored twin virtues of trust and honesty. Fortunately, the vast majority of travelers on the information superhighway possess those virtues.

15

What's Ahead in Entertainment?

Where does the information superhighway in entertainment lead from here? The good news is that the Clinton administration's enthusiasm for new technology that will "wire America" was shared by newly-elected Republicans in Congress early in 1995. However, while the administration announced a $500 million, five-year government spending program in 1994 to encourage American industry to develop the technology necessary for the new information age, the Republicans who came to power the following year prefer private sector financing of the project and not the government.

The bad news is that there are already some "potholes" on the information superhighway. Despite some of the setbacks or problems mentioned in this progress report, there is still much more good news about the future of entertainment technology on the information superhighway. This is shown in new products and services either already started or in the planning stages, such as the following:

Sony Corporation has developed a new process to create digital masters for laser disks and prerecorded videotapes. Officials say it will significantly improve the picture quality of tapes and disks on players consumers already own. Both Sony and Sharp Electronics have created digital video players using disks the same size as audio compact disks that are able to hold full-length motion pictures. The players promise crisper pictures and sound as well as computer capabilities such as random-access searches that will let viewers access any scene in a movie.

Compaq, one of the leading makers of personal computers, is working on a TV set that will share some of the characteristics of computers. A prototype model, called "Mr. PC Head," combines a television, a telephone, a stereo, and computing capabilities.

AT&T, meanwhile, has developed a prototype computerized system that links the telephone to the television. A small system box that sits on the television set permits consumers to display news, traffic, investment information, weather, and electronic mail on TV. It also will offer home banking and shopping information, as such services become available. The system will sell for about $329.

Advances in digital technology are enabling television manufacturers to develop new flat-screen sets that resemble laptop computers. Sony Electronics, meanwhile, has introduced the first computer monitor with a rectangular screen that has the same proportions as a movie theater screen, making it ideal for showing widescreen or "letterbox" movies on computers.

Another exciting development is digital home theater. New laser disks of movies feature an advanced audio system that improves dramatically over present stereo surround sound technology. Called AC-3, Dolby Surround Digital made its debut on the laser disk of the movie *Clear and Present Danger*. The new standard digitally separates channels, approaching the sound in the best audio-equipped theaters. "It really puts you in the center of the action," says Mike Fidler of Pioneer Electronics.

These and other audio and video advancements may take us into a "tricentric world" when all homes will be humming with interactive TVs, videophones, and personal computers. "The digital age has arrived," says Joseph P. Clayton, an executive vice president of Thomson Consumer Electronics. "Consumers are becoming more comfortable with sophisticated electronic

> "The digital age has arrived."

Movies on 5-inch laser disks in digital picture and sound sharpness may further revolutionize home entertainment.
(Photo courtesy I.B.M.)

devices." Thomson, which introduced the first digital satellite TV system in 1994, is already working on incorporating interactive features into satellite reception, as well as into some of the other capabilities of a networked computer.

A joint venture of Thomson and Sun Microsystems will enable people to use their TVs to buy concert tickets, see videos on demand, shop, and do all the things interactive enthusiasts predict. The technology, which requires Sun's computers and Thomson's set-top TV boxes, will be sold to cable, telephone, satellite, and broadcast TV companies.

Sales figures back up many industry officials' confidence in the digital age, according to the Electronic Industries Association.

Americans spent almost as much for home computers in 1994 ($8.07 billion) as they did for television sets ($8.4 billion). Because computers cost considerably more than TV sets, the figures reflect that 6.7 million computers were sold, compared to 25.4 million TV sets.

Many consumer electronics analysts remain skeptical, however, that the personal computer can compete with recreational devices such as video game players. They say that people who play game software on their personal computer are still relatively few in number. This may change with the emerging technology that will enable Nintendo or Sega players to network with other game players via computers—but the change may be slow in coming about. "Social gaming is a horse and buggy story," says Nintendo's Peter Main. "I think we'll ring in the new millennium just starting to see how this is going to work out."

While enthusiasts and skeptics may disagree, the electronics industry reports indicate there is clearly a consumer appetite for home electronics devices that provide both entertainment and information. That increasingly means the introduction of digital devices that convert all text, sound, pictures, and video into a form that can be recorded and played back, transmitted and received, as electronic pulses.

> "The Information Superhighway will evolve as it has been doing for the past 30 years, and maybe by the year 2010, we will call our grandchildren and see them on a videophone."

"There's a lot of momentum building behind new and emerging technologies," said Stan Pinkwas, editor of *Video* magazine. He was one of more than 100,000 industry and media representatives displaying or checking out the latest advances in entertainment technology at the 1995 national Consumer Electronics Show in Las Vegas, Nevada.

America is clearly embracing new entertainment technology, and HDTV, digital, interactive, and multimedia are expected to be important areas of development in the future. However, "Don't expect to wake up one morning and find an on-ramp to the 500-channel information highway at your door," caution technology writers Mike Snider and Bruce Schwartz in *USA Today*. They cite a report from New Networks Institute and Fairfield Research titled "The Information Superhighway: Get a Grip." The report says, "The information highway will evolve as it has been doing for the past 30 years, and maybe by the year 2010, we will call our grandchildren and see them on a videophone."

But most consumers eager to ride on the entertainment road of the information superhighway think more positively. Just think . . . Won't theater-like sound be great on new flat-screen and large-screen television sets like the just-released RCA 80-inch projection TV? It retails for $8,499, but hey, now *that's* entertainment!

16

The Future of the Information Revolution

Where does the information revolution go from here, in science and medicine, business and industry, and education as well as entertainment? It will depend largely on whose investment money is used to develop the technology and offer it to consumers, according to John Markoff, financial writer for the *New York Times*.

The Clinton administration's program introduced three years ago to create the information superhighway and bring it to reality was and still is essential to the nation's half-trillion dollar information technology industry, according to a 1995 report by the National Academy of Sciences.

The federal government is spending $1.1 billion each year on the program, known as the High Performance Computing and Communications Initiative. Markoff reports that the Democrat-sponsored program supports the development of advanced computers and computer networks, which are the foundation of the information superhighway. Republicans who came to power in

Information technology's future on the information superhighway is virtually assured, as millions have welcomed advances in computers and telecommunications. (Photo courtesy I.B.M.)

Congress in 1994 cite the program as one that could be eliminated in order to offset proposed tax cuts. They maintain that much of the investment in the technology to bring about the information superhighway should be from private sources, and that the government should not fund the venture.

Some of the nation's leading computer researchers at corporations and universities argue that government support for research is crucial for the American economy to remain competitive with technological advances in other countries, such as Japan and Germany. A special panel of technology experts recommended that support also be continued for a series of research goals known as the Grand

> "If federal funding is pulled away from development of technology for the information superhighway, it could be decades before the nation realizes what had been lost."

Challenges, difficult scientific problems that are intended to push the limits of computer technology.

"If federal funding is pulled away from development of technology for the information superhighway, it could be decades before the nation realizes what had been lost," says Larry Smarr, director of the National Center for Supercomputer Applications and a member of the committee that prepared the report.

Despite some roadblocks and detours, it is very unlikely that the information superhighway will not be paved. Once it has begun, it is sure to reach the goal its believers intend for it, or something very much like it. It may take more time and money than originally envisioned, but the reason it will become a reality is that Americans—especially young people who are the technology innovators of tomorrow—have always liked and supported what is new and challenging. For that reason alone, the electronic information revolution, already very noticeable in our present, is destined to be an important part of all of our futures.

Glossary

analog information transmission — A method of storing information, typically sound or motion video, as continuously varying wave forms.

bulletin board (computer) — Telecommunications services that allow computer users to send and receive messages.

CD — Compact Disk. An information-recording medium for digital sound.

CD-i — Compact disk with interactive capabilities.

CD-ROM — Compact Disk Read-Only Memory. A 4¾-inch laser- encoded optical disk which stores data but cannot record data.

chip (computer) — A computer circuit built on a small piece, or chip, of semiconductor material.

circuit — A circular stream of electricity.

data — Information that can be processed by a computer.

database — A collection of stored data, sometimes called a database management system, organized so that it can be retrieved in various ways.

digital information transmission — A method of recording information electronically in numeric units.

disk drive — The part of a computer that "reads" the information stored on a disk or "floppy disk."

distance learning	Information that is obtained via telephone, television, computer, or other electronic source that comes from a distant location.
electronic mail ("E-Mail")	Messages sent electronically to and from different computers via the computer network.
fax (facsimile transmission)	An electronic method of sending and receiving printed information. A document is converted into a series of lines of electrical information that is transmitted by telephone.
fiber-optic cable	A cable made from a bundle of fine glass strands over which information is transmitted in the form of an intense beam of light.
graphics	Computer-generated art and illustrations.
hard drive	An internal drive in a computer system unit that houses a permanently installed hard or fixed drive that stores the information put into the computer.
high-definition television (HDTV)	A digital television broadcasting system that can create sharper, clearer pictures than regular television produces.
hologram	A three-dimensional photograph taken by laser.
icon	A small on-screen picture or graphic that symbolizes a specific computer activity or program.
information superhighway	Term used to describe a vast network of shared information via computer, television, satellite, or other forms of communication.
interactive	The ability to offer many choices that result in succeeding scenarios that vary according to the choices made by the operator.
interactive multimedia	Various types of information devices that are presented interactively by a computer in response to user input.

Internet	An international information network accessible by use of a computer, modem, and telephone.
ISDN (Integrated Systems Digital Network)	An international standard for transmission of digital data over telephone lines.
laser	A device that produces a very pure and intense light, used in various ways for information storage and optics.
laser disk	An optical storage disk, typically 12 inches in diameter, that carries video, audio, and text to be played back on a video monitor. Also known as a videodisk.
laser disk player	Like a video recorder (VCR) except that instead of tapes, it plays laser disks that produce sharper images and CD-quality sound, provide swift random playback to any location on the disk, and store vast numbers of images.
letterbox	See WIDESCREEN.
local area network (LAN)	A linked group of computers, typically connected by cables, that supports the sharing of files and applications among users. A school's LAN includes all the computers in the school that are hooked together to share software and administrative tools.
megabytes	A numerical measure of the number of characters the computer can handle at once. Mega means million, and one megabyte equals about 500 pages of text.
modem (modulator-demodulator)	A computer accessory that translates computer data into a series of tones transmitted over telephone lines, for sending and receiving text and graphics.
monitor	A computer screen.

multimedia	The combination of sound, still and moving visuals, and text in one on-screen computer application.
network	A system of interconnected equipment such as radios, telephones, television transmitters, or computers that can communicate with each other and share the same software, information, and related equipment such as printers.
on-line	To be available on a computer network.
RAM (random access memory)	A way to measure how much information the computer's memory can hold and work with.
scanner	A computer accessory that captures images so they can be used in a computer application.
simulations	A multimedia application that is designed to simulate a real-world environment.
software	Computer programs that can perform various tasks.
telecommunications	A means of communicating with people in other locations through use of a combination of computer software, modems, and telephone lines.
teleconferencing	A method by which people in different places are able to communicate via shared television channels.
3DO	A machine similar in appearance to a CD or laser disk player that plays interactive multimedia disks with expanded capabilities of image sharpness and greater animation speed.
virtual reality	Computer or other electronic software that allows the user to experience a simulated environment that he or she seems to physically enter.
wide-area network (WAN)	A network spanning a large geographic area, such as a multi-school district or an entire state. Local area networks can connect to the WAN.

widescreen — Television sets that show movies not in the square format of standard TV screens, but in the wider, "letterbox" ratio seen on movie theater screens.

word processing — Typing and editing manuscripts with a computer, using special software.

Sources

Books

Negroponte, Nicholas. *Being Digital.* New York: Alfred A. Knopf, 1995.

Reports

LINK Resources Corp., New York City, 1995. "Technology in the American Household," Times Mirror Center for the People and the Press, New York City, 1994.

Periodicals

Andrews, Edmund L. "F.C.C. Backs Digital Satellite Radio." *New York Times*, January 13, 1995, p. C3.

Bryant, Adam. "Computer Games with Principles." *New York Times*, Nov. 7, 1993, Sec. 4A, p. 36.

Corliss, Richard. "Rock Goes Interactive." *Time*, January 17, 1994, p. 58.

Corliss, Richard. "Virtual, Man!" *Time*, November 1, 1993, p. 80.

Deutschman, Alan. "Scramble on the Information Highway." *Fortune*, February 7, 1994, p. 129.

Eiser, Leslie. "Edutaining Our Kids." *Technology and Learning*, October 1993, p. 27.

Everett, David. "Putting Filmgoers in the Big Picture." *New York Times*, August 8, 1993, p. B1.

Fisher, Lawrence M. "A New System for Video Games." *New York Times*, June 1, 1994, p. C2.

Flynn, Laurie. "Browsers Make Navigating the World Wide Web a Snap." *New York Times*, January 29, 1995, p. F8.

Goldberg, Ron. "ROM Revolution." *Video*, July 1994, p. 42.

Halverson, Guy. "Cable TV Is Feeling Jolly." *Christian Science Monitor*, December 20, 1994, p. 9.

Harmetz, Aljean. "Two Special Effects." *New York Times*, July 24, 1994, p. H13.

Helyar, John. "A Whole New Ballgame." *Wall Street Journal*, September 9, 1994, p. R-9.

Kantrowitz, Barbara. "Live Wires." *Newsweek*, September 6, 1993, p. 42.

Korman, Ken. "Building a Better Beast." *Video*, November 1994, p. 56.

Lewis, Peter H. "Peering Out a 'Real Time' Window." *New York Times*, February 8, 1995, p. C1.

Mannes, George. "The Incredible Shrinking Videodisk." *Video*, July, 1993, p. 54.

Markoff, John. "Turning the Desktop PC Into a Talk Radio Medium." *New York Times*, March 4, 1993, p. C1.

Maslin, Janet. "Restored 'My Fair Lady' Looks Loverly Once More." *New York Times*, September 21, 1994, p. B3.

McCartney, Scott. "For Teens, Chatting on Internet Offers Comfort of Anonymity." *Wall Street Journal*, December 18, 1994, p. B1.

Negroponte, Nicholas. "What's in It (Multimedia) for Me?" *Modern Maturity*, February-March, 1994, p. 27.

Pargh, Andy. "The Guru Predicts 1995's Hot Products." *Satellite Choice*, January, 1995, p. 331.

Ramirez, Anthony. "A War Within a Single Wire." *New York Times*, October 27, 1993, p. C-2.

Snider, Mike. "New Video Games Push Limits of 16-Bit Format." *USA Today*, December 15, 1994, p. 4D.

Strauss, Bob. "Flight So Fancy." *Entertainment Weekly*, February 10, 1995, p. 72.

Tierney, John. "Will They Sit by the Set, or Ride a Data Highway?" *New York Times*, June 20, 1993, p. 12.

Warren, Rich. "From Basement to Bijou." *Video,* February 1995, p. 22.

Wilson, Kim. "Virtual Reality." *Home Theater*, January 1995, p. 62.

INTERVIEWS

Bird, Nancy. Telephone conversation with director of corporate relations, JVC Company of America, Elmwood Park, NJ, December 27, 1994.

Boswell, Camela. Telephone conversation with public relations associate, LucasArts, San Rafael, Calif., January 10, 1995.

Caron, Andre H. Telephone conversation with director of New Technologies Research Laboratory, University of Montreal, Montreal, Canada, December 14, 1994.

Clayton, Joseph P. Telephone conversation with executive vice president, Thomson Consumer Electronics, Indianapolis, Ind., December 20, 1994.

Coletta, Colleen. Telephone conversation with director of corporate communications, Optical Data Corp., Warren, N.J., July 6, 1994.

Harris, Neil. Telephone conversation with vice president, Simutronics Corp., Gaitherburg, Md., November 11, 1994.

Johnston, Mary. Telephone conversation with press information director, Dream Quest Images, Simi Valley, Calif., January 11, 1995.

Margolis, Albert. Telephone conversation with marketing director, Pioneer Electronics, Long Beach, Calif., October 4, 1994.

Negroponte, Nicholas. Telephone conversation with director of Media Laboratory, Massachusetts Institute of Technology, Cambridge, Mass., January 4, 1995.

Orban, Linda. Telephone conversation with public relations director, Knowledge Adventure, La Crescenta, Calif., January 11, 1995.

Reynolds, Steve. Telephone conversation with interactive media specialist, LINK Resources, New York City, January 5, 1995.

Rhoades, Rick. Telephone conversation with 3DO senior account executive, Bohle Co., Los Angeles, Calif., August 19, 1994.

Rich, Keith J. Telephone conversation with president of Integrated Systems by Rich, Naperville, Ill., January 16, 1995.

Schultz, Carolyn. Telephone conversation with promotions manager, Virtual World Entertainment, Los Angeles, Calif., January 16, 1995.

Silvern, Steven. Telephone conversation with professor of early childhood education, Auburn University, Auburn, Ala., December 1, 1994.

Smith, Robert. Telephone conversation with executive director, Interactive Services Association, Silver Spring, Md., December 5, 1994.

Stonehill, Brian. Telephone conversation with director of media studies, Pomona College, Pomona, Calif., December 7, 1994.

White, Matthew. Telephone conversation with president of MPI Multimedia, Oak Forest, Ill., January 6, 1995.

Wilson, Elizabeth. Telephone conversation with director, media services, Interactive Network, Hayward, Calif., December 6, 1994.

Zumbrunnen, Suzanne. Telephone conversation with marketing coordinator, Showscan Entertainment, Culver City, Calif., January 11, 1995.

INDEX

Italic page numbers indicate illustrations or captions.
Page numbers followed by a "g" indicate glossary terms.

A

AC-3 (Dolby Surround Digital) 104
Academy Awards 69
Acclaim Entertainment (video game company) 30, 31
Aerosmith (rock music group) 81
African American Experience, The: A History (edutainment software) 53
Alaska 63
Alexandria, Virginia 6, 16
Aliens (film) 67
Alien vs. Predator (video game) 40
Alwadish, David J. 90, 91
American Museum of Natural History (New York City) 46
American Telephone & Telegraph Co. (AT&T) 6, 37, 104
America Online 16, 62, 64
Ameritech Corporation 14, 16
analog information transmission 111g
Andrews, Edmund L. 87
Apollo 10 (spacecraft) 10
Apple Computer Inc. ix, 42, 79
Arlen, Gary 95
astronomy 54
Atari (video game maker) 25, 40, 41
Atari Jaguar player 40
Atkinson, George 20
Atlanta, Georgia 49
Atqasuk, Alaska 63

AT&T *see* American Telephone & Telegraph Co.
automatic focus 20

B

Barney's Hide and Seek (video game) 29
baseball 97
basketball 96
BattleTech (video game) 48, *50*
Beaver, Don 63
"Beeper Kid" (monitoring device) 101
Bell Atlantic Corporation 6, 13, 16
Bell South Corporation 14
Betamax (videotape format) 19
Bettman, Gary 93
Binary Zoo (software company) 53
Black Tie White Noise (David Bowie music album) 82
Blade Runner (film) 70
Blockbuster Video 20, 31
BMC-110 BetaMovie (camcorder) 20
Bornstein, Steven 95
Boulder, Colorado 65–66
Boulder High School (Boulder, Colorado) 66
Bowie, David 82
Braun, Jeff 56
Broderbund (software company) 52

Bug Adventure (edutainment software) 56
built-in microphones 20
bulletin boards (computer) 3, 65, 100, 111g
Butterworth, Brent 79

C

cable radio 88
cable TV 5–6, 10, 13–15, 31, 83
California *see also* Virtual World
   home theaters 75
   interactive TV 13, 16
   Internet broadcasting 81
   special effects 69
   virtual reality 46
caller-ID 14
camcorders 20, 64
Canada 15, 16, 93
Carmen Sandiego *see* Where in Space Is Carmen Sandiego?; Where in the World Is Carmen Sandiego?
Caron, Andre H. 15
Carrey, Jim 70, 71
Carson, Johnny 10
Cartoon History of the Universe (edutainment software) 59
Case, Steve 63
Castle of Dr. Brain (edutainment software) 53
Castro Valley, California 16
Catholic Church 100
CD (compact disk) 111g *see also* photo CDs
CD-i (Interactive Compact Disk System) 38–39, 79, 81, 82, 111g
CD-ROM (compact disk-read only memory) 34, 58, 111g *see also* DVD (digital video disk)
   computers equipped with drives for 2
   full-length films on 7

interactive systems with 35–36
   music on 81, 82, 84
cellular radios 62
Centennial Middle School (Boulder, Colorado) 65
Chicago, Illinois 16, 49, 96
"Child Guardian" (monitoring device) 101
"Child Sentry" (monitoring device) 101
chip (computer) 111g
CinemaScope (film technology) 44
Cinerama (film technology) 44
Cinesite (film restoration company) 71, 72
Cinetropolis (multi-attraction center in Ledyard, Connecticut) 45, 47
circuit 111g
citizens band (CB) radios 62
Clayton, Joseph P. 12, 104
Clear and Present Danger (film) 104
Clegg, Almon 91
Clinton, Bill vii, 103, 108
Colorado 16, 65–66
colorization of films 72
color restoration 71
commercials 5, 15
Commodore 64 (personal computer) 25
Compaq Computer Corporation 104
CompuServe (on-line service) 16, 62, 64
computers *see also* Apple Computer Inc.; Internet; on-line
   bulletin boards 3, 65, 100, 111g
   chip 111g
   companies 34, *34, 35,* 104
   computer-television battle 6–8
   edutainment software 52–60
   future of 110
   games 34–35, 41–43, *42, 43*
   IBM models 41
   Macintosh models 41, 69

monitor 104, 113g
movies on demand 22–23
multimedia 2, 7, 33, 34
music software 82–83
privacy and security 99
"set-top computers" 41
Silicon Graphics models 69, 70, 71
special effects *68, 69*
sports computer 97
statistics 3, 106
Video Toaster *68, 69*
Windows 41, 64
Congress, U.S. 90, 103, 109
Connecticut 16, 45, 47
Consumer Electronics Show (Las Vegas, Nevada, 1995) 41, 106
Corliss, Richard 82
Cotton Bowl (Dallas, Texas) 80
"Coupon Radio" (car radio system) 90, 91
Cox Cable 16
Crow, The (film) 67, 69–70
Cruising World (magazine) 96
Crunch Media 82
Crystal Dynamics 38, *38*

D

Dallas, Texas 65, 80
data 111g
database 111g
data superhighway *see* information superhighway
Davidson (software company) 53
Denver, Colorado 16
digital audio radio (D.A.R.) 87
Digital Cable Radio *87,* 87–88
digital camcorders 20
digital cash 100–101
digital compositing 70
digital home theaters 104
digital information transmission 111g
digital recording pianos 83

digital satellite radio 86
Digital Satellite System (DSS) 5, *10,* 11–12
"digital theme park" *47,* 48
Digital VCR Conference 21
digital video disk *see* DVD (digital video disk)
Dinosaur Adventure (edutainment software) 58
DirecTV (satellite television service) 94
Discovery (space shuttle) 61
disk drive 111g
Disklavier concert grand piano 83–84
distance learning 112g
Dolby noise reduction 19
Donkey Kong (video game) 31
Doom (video game) 40
Dracula (film) 39
Dream Quest Images (special effects company) 69, 70
DSS *see* Digital Satellite System
DVD (digital video disk) 21, 22, *22,* 103–104
Dynamic Digital Sound 46

E

EA (software company) 38
East Asia 88
Eastman Kodak Company 71
eavesdropping 101
EduQuest (software company) 52–53
edutainment (education + entertainment) 52–60
8-bit video game player 2, 25
800 Video Computer System (video game system) 25
Eiser, Leslie 53
Eisner, Michael 14
electronic home management systems 77–78
Electronic Industries Association 19, 105

INDEX 123

electronic mail ("E-Mail") 6, 63, 112g
electronic money 100
electronic newspapers 33
electronic view-finders 20
E-Mail *see* electronic mail
ESPN (cable network) 8
Europe 88
Ezra, Jack 21

F

"factoids" *48,* 49
Fairfield Research 107
fax (facsimile transmission) 6, 112g
Federal Communications Commission (FCC) 13, 86
Felt, David 56
fiber-optic cable 112g
Fidler, Mike 104
FIFA International Soccer (computer game) 38
films *see* movies
flat-screen TV sets 104
Florida 6, 17, 83
football 94, 95, 96
France viii
"full digital synergy" 37
Full Service Network 17

G

Galvin, Mark 70
Game Boy (handheld video game player) 2, 40
Game Gear (handheld video game player) 2
Gear Works (video game) 29
"Geek of the Week" (Radio Internet feature) 90
General Instrument Corporation 13
Georgia 49
Germany viii, 109
Gex (computer game) 38

giant-screen theaters 45
girls *see* women
Godfrey, Arthur 9
Gold Star Company Limited 37
golf 94–95, 96–97
Golf Channel (television channel) 94–95
Golf World (magazine) 96
"go-motion" process 68
Gore, Al vii
Grand Challenges (research goals) 109–110
graphics 112g
Grateful Dead (rock music group) 82
Great Britain 21
Gross, Bill 57, 58
guitars 82, 83
Guns N' Roses (rock music group) 82

H

Hamill, Mark 42
ham radio operators 62
handheld video game players 2
"handoff" function 91
hang-gliding 96
hard drive 112g
Harris, Robert A. 71
Hartford, Connecticut 16
Hatboro, Pennsylvania 87–88
HBO (cable channel) 5
HDTV *see* high-definition television
HD VCRs *see* high-definition video cassette recorders
Helyar, John 93, 94
high-definition television (HDTV) 12–13, 21, 112g
high-definition video cassette recorders (HD VCRs) 20, 21
High Performance Computing and Communications Initiative 108
Hilton Hotel (Chicago, Illinois) 3
Hitachi Limited 20
hologram 112g

home shopping 5, 6, 17
Home Theater (magazine) 78
home theaters 73–78, *75*
Hook (film) 39
Horner, Jack 68
horoscopes 15
Houston, Texas 49
hyper-linking 64

I

IBM computers 41
icon 112g
Illinois 76
Illusion of Gaia (video game) 29
ILM *see* Industrial Light and Magic
Imax (giant-screen film company) 45, 46
Industrial Light and Magic (ILM) 67, 70, 71
information superhighway vii–ix, 103, 108–110, 112g *see also* Internet; on-line
"Information Superhighway, The: Get a Grip" (New Networks Institute and Fairfield Research report) 107
Integrated Systems by Rich (home theater contractor) 76
interactive 112g
Interactive Digital Software Association 29
interactive game-playing machines 8
interactive home shopping 14
interactive multimedia 32–43, 112g
Interactive Multiplayer 37
interactive music technology 79–85
Interactive Network (cable TV service) 16
interactive satellite video 92–93
interactive sports technology 92–97
interactive technology 32–43
interactive television 13–17, 96
Interactive TV (cable TV service) 94

Internet 56, 61–65, 80, 88–89, 101–102, 113g
Internet Multicasting Company 89
"Internet record stores" 81
"Internet Talk Radio" (computer-based radio show) 89
Internet Underground Music Archive 81
Into the Deep (3-D Imax film) 46
Isaac Asimov's Science Adventure II (edutainment software) 57
ISDN (Integrated Systems Digital Network) 113g
Iwerks Entertainment 45

J

Jackson, Janet 82
Jagger, Mick 80
Jaminator (music software) 82–83
Japan viii, 21, 49, 109
"Jeopardy!" (TV show) 15, 16
Jersey City, New Jersey 46
Joe Montana's NFL Football (video game) 96
Jones, Ed 72
"Jump: David Bowie Interactive" (music software) 82
Jurassic Park (film) 37–38, 67–69
JVC/Victor Company of Japan Limited 19, 40

K

Kano (video game character) 27–28
Kantrowitz, Barbara 63
karaoke (music technology) 83, *84*
Katz, James C. 71
Kennedy Center for the Performing Arts (Washington, D.C.) 90
Knowledge Adventure (software company) 56, 57, 58

L

LAN *see* local area network
Lantieri, Michael 67
laser 113g
Laser Active Multi-Format Player 36
laser disk 104, *105,* 113g
laser disk player 2, 74, 113g
LaserKaraoke (music disks) 37
Last Buffalo, The (3-D Imax film) 46
Las Vegas, Nevada 49
Latin America 88
Lawrence of Arabia (film) 71
LCD (liquid crystal display) stereo eyeglasses 18
Ledyard, Connecticut 45
Lee, Brandon 67, 69, 70
Lessons from History: A Celebration of Blackness (edutainment software) 53
letterbox (film format) 113g *see also* widescreen
Lewis, Peter H. 61, 64
Liberty Science Center (Jersey City, New Jersey) 46
Liberty Sports (cable TV channel) 97
LightWave 3D (graphics software) *68, 69*
LINK Resources Corporation 1, 9
local area network (LAN) 113g
Lockwood, Bryan 63
Lopiano, Donna 97
Los Angeles, California 46
lottery 15
Lucas, George 34, 67
LucasArts (computer games company) 34, *34,* 35
Luke Skywalker (computer game character) 34
Lundgren, Todd 82
Luxor hotel (Las Vegas, Nevada) 49
Lynx (handheld video game player) 2

M

Macintosh computers 41, 69
Madden, John 29
Magnavox Company 25
Main, Peter 106
Main Street Books (software company) 59
Manhattan (borough of New York City) 46
Marin County, California 75
Mario Is Missing (edutainment software) 53
Markoff, John 88, 89, 108
Mars (planet) 54–55
Maryland 13–14
Mask, The (film) 70–71
Massachusetts Institute of Technology (Cambridge, Massachusetts) 100
Matador (photo imaging software) 70
Matsushita Electric Industrial Company Limited 37
Maxis (software company) 54, 55, 56
M-bone (Internet broadcasting technology) 61–62
MCA Incorporated 37
McCartney, Scott 65
McCormick Place (exhibition hall in Chicago, Illinois) 3
Media Laboratory (Massachusetts Institute of Technology, Cambridge, Massachusetts) 7
megabytes 113g
Metallica (rock music group) 82
Mexico 88
Microsoft Corporation 7–8, 23, 64, 84, 100
Midnight Raiders (video game) *27*
Mighty Morphin Power Rangers (video game) *28*
miniaturization 41
modem (modulator-demodulator) 3, 6, 113g

Modern Maturity (magazine) 32
monitor (computer screen) 104, 113g
Montana, Joe *see* Joe Montana's NFL Football (video game)
Montgomery County, Maryland 14
Montreal, Canada 15
Moon 10, 55
Mortal Kombat (video game) 27, 31
Mortal Kombat II (video game) 30
motion simulation 45
mountain biking 96
Movie Plex (on-line service) 63
movies
   movies-on-demand 14, 17, 22–23
   restoration 71–72
   special effects 67–72
   widescreen 13, 104, 115g
"Mr. PC Head" (TV/computer prototype) 104
multimedia 3, 8, 32–43, 114g
multimedia personal computers 2, 7
"Murder, She Wrote" (TV show) 16
Muren, Dennis 67
MUSE analog signal 21
museums 39
music 37, 79–85, *84*
My Fair Lady (film) 71
Mystery at the Museum (edutainment software) 53

N

Naperville, Illinois 76
National Academy of Sciences 108
National Association of Broadcasters 87
National Football League 94
National Press Club 90
Naturemax Theater (American Museum of Natural History, New York City) 46
NBA Jam (video game) 29
NBC (TV network) 10

NEC Corporation 25
Negroponte, Nicholas 7, 32–33, 89, 100
Nelson, Doreen 55
"nerds" 4
NES *see* Nintendo Entertainment System
network 114g *see also* Internet; on-line
Nevada 41, 49, 106
New Jersey 13, 46
Newleaf Entertainment 31
New Networks Institute 107
news-on-demand 17
newspapers, electronic *see* electronic newspapers
Newsweek (magazine) 63
New Technologies Research Laboratory (University of Montreal) 15
New York City *see* Manhattan (borough of New York City); Queens, New York
New York Times (newspaper) 61, 80
New York Times/CBS News Poll 15, 17
New York Times Company 96
Nintendo (video game company) 5, 25, 34, 41, 106
Nintendo Entertainment System (NES) 25, 37
nitrate film 72
Notebaert, Richard C. 14
No World Order (CD-i music game) 82

O

Odyssey (video game) 25
Omaha, Nebraska 16
on-line 114g
on-line communications 3, *4, 59,* 61–66, 96
Oracle Corporation 23
Orlando, Florida 6, 17, 83

■ ■ ■
INDEX 127

P

Pacific Telesis 13
Page, Parker 30
Palo Alto, California 81
Panasonic Company 21, 37, 38
Pasadena, California 49
pay-per-view service 5
pay-radio service 88
Penguin Astronomy Dictionary 55
Pennsylvania 87–88
Pentium (microchip) 41
"personalization" 33
Philips Electronics 21, 38, 39, 79, 84
phone services 14
"phonevision" 14
photo CDs 37, 39
pianos 83–84
Pinkwas, Stan 106
Pioneer Corporation 22, 36
pirated software 100
"player in command" technology 31
PlayStation (interactive system) 40–41
polls and surveys
 computer use 3
 privacy and safety concerns 99
 television use 4, 5, 10
 VCR and videotape use 19
 video game use 26
premium services (cable TV) 5–6
Presley, Elvis 82
PrimeStar (satellite TV system) 12
Prismon, John 66
privacy 99, 99–100, 102
Prodigy (on-line service) 3, 8, 62, 64
projection television sets 74, *74,* 107
Provenzo Jr., Eugene 30
puzzle or problem-solving games 53

Q

Queens, New York 6
QuickTime VR (virtual reality software) 42

R

radio 33, 86–91
radio data system (R.D.S.) 90–91
Radio Internet 90
Radio Technology for Mankind (Internet radio station) 90
RAM (random access memory) 114g
Ranum, Marcus 101
rating systems 29
RCA Corporation 11, 19
R.D.S. *see* radio data system
Rebel Assault (computer game) 35
record companies 81
Red Planet (video adventure) 49
Redshift (edutainment software) 54–55
remote-control pads 16
renting from home 23, 31
"reproducing piano" 83
Republican Party 103, 108, 109
Reynolds, Steve 17
Rich, Keith 77, 78
Richards, Keith 80
Road Rash (computer game) 38
Roberts, Ty 82
Robin Hood: Prince of Thieves (film) 70
Robocop (film) 69
Rolling Stones (rock music group) 80, 81
Roman Catholic Church 100
Rosetto, Louis 99
Rotisserie (baseball computer) 97
R360 (video adventure) 49–50
R3000 (microprocessor) 41
Rundgren, Todd 79–80

S

Saffo, Paul 89
Sailing World (magazine) 96
Samurai Showdown (video game) *38*
San Diego, California 49

satellite radio broadcasting 86–87
satellite television broadcasting 5, 6, 10–11, *11, 12,* 94
Saugerties, New York 79
scanner 114g
schools 53–54, *54*
Schulhof, Michael P. 88
Schwartz, Bruce 107
Seattle, Washington 23
Secret of Monkey Island, The (video game) 29
Sega (video game company)
   game-playing systems 25, 34, 39, 40, 41
   home electronic delivery systems 31
   network game playing 106
   sports games *94, 95,* 96
   virtual reality games 49
Sega Channel, The (cable and satellite television channel) 31
Sega Genesis (video game system) 26, *26,* 31, 36, 40
Semsky, Arnie 16
"set-top computers" 41
Severe Tire Damage (rock music group) 81
sexual themes 29, 30
Sharp Electronics 103
Sheff, David 27–30
Showscan Entertainment 45, *45,* 46, 50–51
Showtime (cable TV service) 5, 80
Sierra On-Line 53
Silicon Graphics computers 69, 70, 71
Silvern, Steven 29
Sim City (edutainment software) 55–56
SimCity 2000 (video game) 29
simulations 114g
6mm videocassette 23

16-bit video game players 2, 25, 31, 34
64-bit video game players 31, 34, 38, 40
Skyline High School (Dallas, Texas) 65
Skywalker Ranch (Marin County, California) 75
Smarr, Larry 110
"smart card" 91
SNET (telephone company) 16
Snider, Mike 107
Snow Country (magazine) 96
Snow White and the Seven Dwarfs (film) 71, 72
software 114g
Software Toolworks 53
Songer, Nancy 65
Sonic the Hedgehog (video game character) 27
Sony Corporation
   compact digital video disk 21
   digital masters 103
   digital radio 87
   futuristic theater in Manhattan 46
   interactive music 84
   VCRs and videotapes 19, 20
   video game systems 40, 41
Sony Electronics 104
Sony Imagesoft 39
Southwestern Bell Corporation 14
Soviet Union 54
special effects (film) 67–72
Spence, Jonathan 59–60
Spielberg, Steven 37, 67
sports 15, 29, 92–97
Sportslab Inc. 95–96
Sports/Leisure Magazines Group 96
Stahnke, Wayne 83
"Star Trek" (TV show) 66
Star Trek: The Next Generation Interactive Technical Manual (computer game) 41–42, *42, 43*

■ ■ ■
INDEX 129

Star Wars (film series) 34, 35
stereo TV broadcasts 10
Stereo-Visors (LCD viewing eyeglasses) 18
Stonehill, Brian 30
Strauss, Neil 80, 81
Sullivan, Ed 9
Sulski, Jim 77
Summer Consumer Electronics Show (Chicago, Illinois, 1995) 3
"Sunday Ticket" (satellite TV service) 94
Sun Microsystems 105
"superhighway robbery" 102
Super Mario (video game character) 27
Super Mario Brothers (video game) 25
Super Mario Paint (video game) 40
Super Nintendo (video game system) 30, 40
Super Punch-Out (video game) 40
Super Street Fighter II Turbo (computer game) 38
Surreal Field (music technology exhibit) 79
surround sound systems 74
synthesizers 82

T

talk radio 88–90
TCI *see* Tele-Communications Inc.
Technology & Learning (magazine) 53
"Technology in the American Household" (Times Mirror Center study) 3
telecommunications 114g
Tele-Communications Inc. (TCI) 6, 16, 31
teleconferencing 114g
telephone industry 13
telephones 16, 62, 104
television
    3-D 17–18

cable 5–6, 10, 13–15, 31, 83
color 1–2, 9
flat-screen sets 104
high-definition 12–13, 21, 112g
interactive 13–17, 96
new technologies 104
projection sets 74, *74*, 107
satellite broadcasting 5, 6, 10–11, *11, 12*, 94
software delivery over 7
statistics 4–5, 6, 9–18, 10, 106
tennis 96
Tennis (magazine) 96
Terminator 2: Judgment Day (film) 67
Tetris 2 (video game) 29
Texas 49, 65, 80
theft 101–102
32-bit video game players 31, 34, 40
Thomson Consumer Electronics 11, 104–105 *see also* Digital Satellite System (DSS)
3-D Body Adventure (edutainment software) 56
3DO interactive video game player *37,* 37–38, *38,* 41, 114g
3-D TV 17–18
3D TV Corporation 18
THX (home theater consultant) 75
TIE Fighter (computer game) 35
Tierney, John 14
"Tiger" (media-on-demand software) 23
Tilton, Rik 63
Time (magazine) 82
Times Mirror Center for the People and the Press *see* polls and surveys
Time Warner Cable 17, 87
Time Warner Incorporated 6, 22, 31, 37, 83, 87
Tin Star (video game) 40
Tippett, Phil 67
"Todd Pod" (interactive stage set) 80

■ ■ ■
130 ENTERTAINMENT

Toms River, New Jersey 13
"Tonight Show" (TV show) 10
Toshiba Corporation 22
transponder equipment 11
travel assistance 14
Triple D Publishing 78
Trumbull, Douglas 47
trust 101, 102
TurboGrafx-CD game player 37
TV *see* television
TV Guide (magazine) 27
2001: A Space Odyssey (film) 47

U

Ultra 64 (video game system) 40
Unet 2 Corporation (electronic publisher) 96
Universal (computer game) 38
Universal Citywalk (simulator theater in Los Angeles, California) 46
Universal Studios (Hollywood, California) 69
urban planning 55–56
USA Today (newspaper) 107
US West (communications company) 6

V

VCRs and videotapes 2, 5, 6, 19–24, 74
VHS (Video Home System) (videotape format) 19
Viacom International Incorporated 16
Video (magazine) 79
video arcades *40*, 47
video chess 15
video conferencing 6
video E-Mail 63
video game players 2, 25–41, *37*, 106 *see also specific players (e.g., Sega Genesis)*

video games 6, 17, 25–31, 32–43, *38 see also specific games (e.g., Mortal Kombat)*
Video Games: A Guide for Savvy Parents (David Sheff) 27
video servers 23
Video Station (video store franchise) 20
video stores 5, 20
video telephone 16, 62
Video Toaster (computer hardware) *68, 69*
Videoway (cable TV service) 15, 93
Viking (spacecraft) 55
Vineon (graphics software) 71
violence 29, 30
Virginia 6, 16
"virtual community" 64
Virtual Formula Racing (video adventure) 50
Virtual Graceland (music software) 82
Virtual Guitar (music software) 83
virtual reality 44–51, *49*, 114g
Virtual World (Walnut Creek, California theme park) *47, 48*, 48–49, *50*
voice mail 14

W

Wall Street Journal, The (newspaper) 65, 93
Walt Disney Company 14, 63, 71
WAN *see* wide-area network
Warren, Rich 75–76
Washington State 23
weather reports 15
"Wheel of Fortune" (TV show) 16
Where in Space Is Carmen Sandiego? (computer game) 52
Where in the World Is Carmen Sandiego? (computer game) 29, 52, 53, 60

Who Framed Roger Rabbit (film) 67
wide-area network (WAN) 114g
widescreen (letterbox) (TV format) 13, 104, 115g
Windows (computer operating system) 41, 64
Windy City Golf (virtual reality golf course) 96–97
Wing Commander III: Heart of the Tiger (computer/CD-ROM game) 42–43
Winston, Stan 67, 68
women 3, 30–31, 97
Women's Sports Network (cable TV channel) 97
Woodstock '94 (rock concert) 79–80
word processing 115g
World Wide Web (Internet service) 64

X

Xerox PARC (Palo Alto, California) 81
X'EYE system (interactive compact disk system) 40
X-Wing (video game) 34–35, *35, 36*

Y

Yamaha Motor Company Limited 83

Z

Zoo Keeper (edutainment software) 53
zoom lens 20
ZoomScape (interactive movie technology) 57–58
Zumbrunne, Suzanne 50